THE WAY OF THE
WITCH

Dedicated to the Highest Good,
to the Mother and to my magical son LJ

First edition published as *The Wiccan Way* in 2003.

Published in 2020 by Red Wheel Books
An imprint of Red Wheel/Weiser, LLC
with offices at:
65 Parker Street, Suite 7
Newburyport, MA 01950
www.redwheelweiser.com

Text © Sally Morningstar 2020

Design and specially commissioned illustrations
© Welbeck Non-Fiction Limited, part of Welbeck
Publishing Group Limited 2020

Illustrations by Lisa O'Malley

ISBN 978-1-59003-516-0

Printed in Dubai

10 9 8 7 6 5 4 3 2 1

THE WAY OF THE
WITCH

A PATH TO SPIRITUALITY
AND SELF-EMPOWERMENT

SALLY MORNINGSTAR

Red Wheel

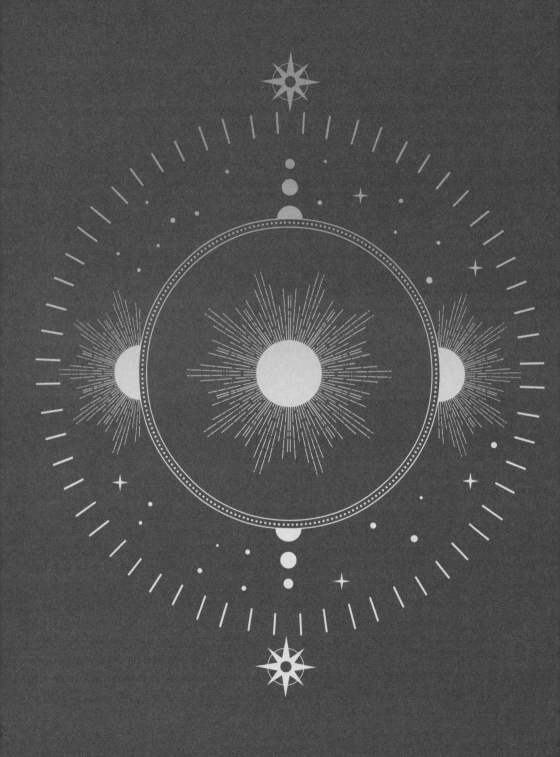

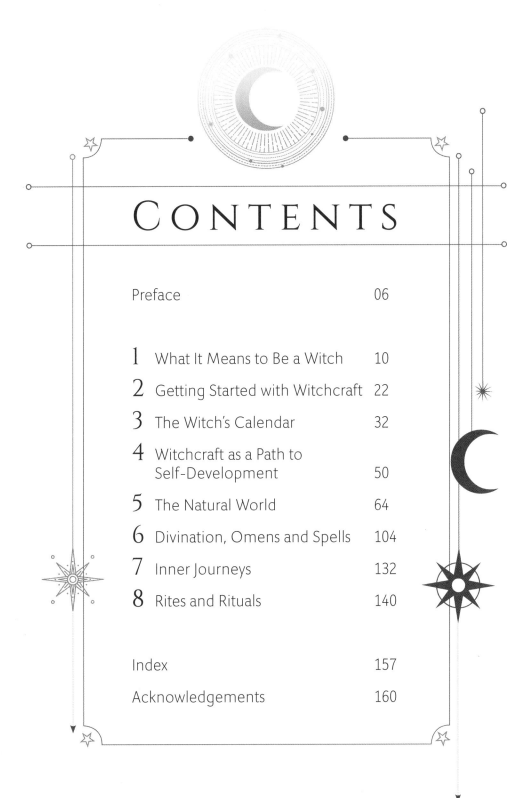

CONTENTS

Preface

This book provides a beautifully simple introduction to witchcraft as a spiritual practice that gives you lots of step-by-step advice and guidance on the Craft. It will help give you a clear understanding of how to live your life following the witchcraft principles of honouring the earth, the natural world, yourself and others. What is little described in witchcraft is that self-development is an integral part of a witch's path – the more evolved the being, the greater their magical potential will be.

Witchcraft is an ancient nature and fertility religion. In our deep historical past, respecting nature was necessary for survival. Communities thrived or died based upon the availability of food, water and shelter. The continuation of life depended on the ability to hunt and find food. With this in mind, it is easy to understand the reasons why people since ancient times have venerated the natural world. Nature was like a mother to our ancestors because she provided all of their needs. The four Greater Sabbats (pagan agricultural festivals) of Imbolc, Beltaine, Lughnasadh and Samhain were established to help the Mother to turn the wheel of creation and thus enact the continuation of life on Earth.

Today that wheel is being compromised because those in control of modern society often disregard the natural world. Witchcraft helps us to work cooperatively with nature and with the forces of creation so that we can live in peace, joy and harmony with each other. With witchcraft we can connect to our rightful place on the earth as guardians of the planet, not abusers, exploiters or violators.

This book explains many witchcraft practices and beliefs, including the background to the Craft, the magical tools, the arrangement of an altar and how to perform rituals and ceremonies. Guidelines are also given to help you develop yourself spiritually, so that you can embody the powers of nature within your own being. Many people assume that witchcraft simply comprises spells, bells and charm bags. It is far more profound than this, for it can provide the link between our own essence and the essence of creation. In witchcraft we believe that the Goddess is the creator and the Horned God her consort. The Horned God represents the divine masculine in witchcraft, who stands in service and protection over the Goddess and the natural world. He has nothing whatsoever to do with a devil or Satan – both of which are of Christian origin.

When we honour the natural world and the powers of creation in a rightful way, we are given the most wondrous gift from the Mother Goddess – her magic. This magic is beyond mortal words. It is the space between, the moment beyond. It opens our eyes to the most glorious truth and evolves our spirit to the point that it is free, happy and at peace.

That magic is only a moment away. If we only had the eyes to see it and the heart to feel it, we would be aware that it is around us and within us all the time. This book aims to help you to find that magical dimension, that natural way of being that brings such joy to the spirit, so that at last you can discover the magic of who you really are and celebrate a unique journey back to yourself.

In addition, this book gives guidance on the practical applications of the Craft in daily life – offering details on healing, psychic protection, rights of passage and finding your magical name. It explains spellcrafting and making your own ritual equipment but, most important of all, it takes you on the journey back to your spirit, to your heart, and to your essence.

I hope you enjoy this book. May it reveal your own beauty to you and show you the Way.

— •☾☀ DEFINITIONS OF COMMON TERMS ☀☽• —

ATHAME	a witch's sacred dagger
THE BOOK OF SHADOWS	a witch's sacred book
COVEN	a group of witches under the guidance of a high priestess
DEVA	a flower spirit
DRYAD	a tree spirit
ESBAT	a coven meeting; less formal than a Sabbat
GAIA	Ancient Greek earth goddess
GNOMES	elemental spirits of the earth element
HORNED GOD	the primary male deity of witchcraft
LEMNASCATE	a symbol of eternity, drawn like a figure of eight
LIBATION	a fluid offering made to a deity
MOTE	'may' or 'shall' (for example, 'So mote it be!' meaning 'May it be so!' or 'So shall it be!')
PSYCHISM	psychic ability and perception
SACRED CIRCLE	a sacred area in which formal ritual working is performed
SAGE SMUDGE STICK	bundled herbal stick of sage leaves
SALAMANDERS	elemental spirits of the fire element
SAMHAIN	(pronounced 'sow-en') the festival of remembering the ancestors, marking the end of the Celtic year and the dawning of the new year, and honouring the last of the current year's harvest festivals
SKYCLAD	naked
STANG	a 'Y'-shaped, forked stick that represents the Horned God
SYLPHS	elemental spirits of the air element
UNDINE	elemental spirits of the water element

WHAT IT MEANS
TO BE A WITCH

'Blessed be!' Traditional Witch's Saying

To be a witch is to venerate the Goddess and her consort, the Horned God, and to follow the ethics and practices of the Old Religion. This ancient pagan tradition existed long before the establishment of the Church. Neo-pagan Wicca (which emerged in the 1950s) is based upon what is still known or understood about the Old Religion but, because of witchcraft's turbulent history, a great deal has been lost. As we really only have mostly modern Wiccan practices to refer to today, this book is largely based around modern-day witchcraft, or Wicca. Fundamentally, both mean the same thing. The term 'Wiccan' usually describes a modern practitioner, whereas a 'witch' implies someone who is 'of the blood' – a traditional witch, who may be able to trace their lineage back hundreds of years through traditional witchcraft covens. However, whether you call yourself a Wiccan or a witch is entirely up to you.

Witchcraft honours the Earth as our spiritual mother (the Goddess) and the sky and the wildness of nature as our spiritual father (the Horned God). In practice this means that we venerate nature and the planet upon which we live. We endeavour not to harm anyone or anything because to us these are all our brothers and sisters with an equal right to exist. Witchcraft is a tradition that works to harm none in thought, word or deed. Anyone, therefore, who says they are a witch but works otherwise should not be considered an authentic practitioner.

Witchcraft is classified as a religion because it has a deity, the Goddess, as its figurehead. It is still the only spiritual tradition that raises the female above the male, in contrast to patriarchal religions such as Christianity and Judaism. As it venerates a goddess, witchcraft follows the moral values associated with feminine spiritual powers, such as love, peace and joy. Witches work by peaceful means, seeking to unite rather than to divide, to be of service to our communities and to be the healers, counsellors and the guardians of all life on the Earth. This is because we see ourselves as the children of the Goddess and the Horned God, who we venerate. When we acknowledge this truth within us, we can only ever love and look after what they have so lovingly created for us.

A Brief History of Witchcraft

It is thought that the term 'witch' originates from the Anglo-Saxon word *wicce* (pronounced 'witcha'), believed to be the basis for the current pronunciation of our modern word 'witch'. It was re-popularized as the term 'Wicca' (pronounced 'wicker') to describe neo-pagan witchcraft in the 1950s.

Witchcraft has had a stormy past. It has been an object of much malice and hostility, largely based upon hysteria and fabrication. Calling someone a witch was at one time enough to condemn them, so that term quickly became a way to brand absolutely any passing innocent as evil. What was overlooked was the fact that at no point has there been a devil in witchcraft, much less any concept of evil or sin. Satan is, in fact, a Christian demon. Yet because of hundreds of years of propaganda against witchcraft, even today people have a primal fear about it being evil and can easily blame it for all sorts of ills.

Witches, pagans and heathens have all been treated as heretics (a term used to define those whose views opposed the Church) throughout the centuries. It is difficult, therefore, to write a definitive history of witchcraft and, because of persecution, much of this important history has been lost or destroyed. However, we know that there was veneration of the feminine from 27,000 years ago because our prehistoric ancestors carved female fertility figurines known as 'the Venuses'. Going back 15,000 years, cave paintings also reveal that the people in our past connected magically with animals and the power of nature.

Witchcraft existed peacefully in various guises for thousands of years. It was not until metal was forged into the sword that a great deal of bloody and aggressive cultural upheaval began across the globe, with battles, conquests and invasions. Warrior gods were venerated, and it did not take long before one vengeful almighty god (Jehovah or Yahweh) was created to reflect the beliefs of this warrior class. Many innocents have suffered throughout the ages because of religion. Members of the peasant classes of the Middle Ages (who were the midwives, herbalists, counsellors and healers of the time) were singled out for discrimination, whether they were actually witches or not.

Witchcraft itself went underground in order to survive and emerged again in Europe in the 1950s after the repeal of the Witchcraft Act. This means that it has been only within the last seventy years or so that witches have legally and safely been able to announce their presence again.

WITCHCRAFT TODAY

Witchcraft in any era is about veneration of nature – this will never change because it is one of its defining principles.

Modern witchcraft – termed British Traditional Wicca – emerged in the 1950s through Gardnerian Wicca founded by Gerald Gardner with Doreen Valiente as his high priestess, Alexandrian Wicca (founded by Alex and Maxine Sanders) and Seax Wicca founded by Raymond Buckland. Other branches of witchcraft established themselves throughout the late twentieth century with Dianic, Feri and Stregheria. There are more but the ones mentioned here are the most well-known.

This means that modern witchcraft has many varied practices, including traditional, Gardnerian, Alexandrian, Celtic, Faery, Seax, Dianic, solitary and hereditary. Although they provide different 'flavours', all varieties venerate the feminine above the masculine. They also all honour the witchcraft rule to 'harm none' and to work for the highest good to the best of their ability.

Modern witchcraft was established through a coven system. A coven is a gathering of witches, led by a high priestess and assisted by her high priest. A coven meets for the Sabbats and at lunar esbats, both of which are explained in more detail later in the book (*see* The Witch's Calendar, *pages 32–49*).

Witchcraft is a tradition of freedom and as such you should always feel free to be yourself. If you would like to know more, there is plenty of information available about the different witchcraft traditions and I would urge you to explore more than one source of information in order to get the most rounded view of each of them.

To be a witch today you can still choose to be coven-based or solitary, initiated or uninitiated, traditional or eclectic. You may well be what is called a 'blood witch' meaning someone who has been drawn to the Craft life after life – 'once a witch, always a witch'.

Whatever path you choose – thanks to the will of our ancestors, the way of the witch remains there for all to tread, as it has for thousands of years.

The Solitary Witch and the Hedgewitch

Although modern witchcraft was founded upon a coven system, this does not preclude solitary witches from following the Craft. In fact, it is more likely that a witch will practise alone these days, as perhaps there are no covens near them or they would prefer to practice alone. Covens tend to be ceremonial or ritual based, and coven practices can sometimes feel limiting to those wishing to be more directly involved with nature.

A solitary witch today is more likely to be traditional, hereditary, eclectic, or Seax (because Seax does include the solitary). But this is where things get complicated because witchcraft today is diverse, decentralized and open to personal interpretation and, as such, there are no clearly defined boundaries as to who is what or what is right or wrong within its interpretations and practices – except for traditional witchcraft whose practices seldom change.

A solitary witch can choose to follow one particular branch of witchcraft. Practising it alone rather than in a group, they can develop their own means and methods of honouring the ways of the witch as it makes sense to them. Some people may feel drawn to working in groups, with altars, magical tools and rituals; others may not. This is where the hedgewitch come in.

Although not historically associated with witchcraft because it is a way of life rather than a religion, hedgewitchcraft tends to gently entwine itself around certain witchcraft practices, such as following the pagan Wheel of the Year, and so it could be true to say that it is loosely included as part of witchcraft today.

A hedgewitch has a deep connection with nature and the natural world, working closely with all levels of creation, from the seen to the unseen. In this way it could be considered more shamanic than other witchcraft practices. Hedgewitches often consider themselves to be 'different' to others and tend to have had particular life experiences that have led them down a solitary path, which is usually where they would like to remain.

The hedgewitch's path is free from doctrine and so individuals can explore, learn, expand and grow by learning from and giving to nature and the natural world in whatever ways make sense to them.

As a hedgewitch myself, I wrote The Hedgewitch's Prayer (*see opposite*), which I repeat when I am entering landscapes or visiting places, to both raise my vibrations and to state the reason why I am there.

THE HEDGEWITCH'S PRAYER

1. Stand quietly, eyes closed, with your right hand on your right breast (the home of the spiritual heart).

2. Breathe deeply and calmly for a few moments, with both feet on the ground.

3. Repeat The Hedgewitch's Prayer:
   'I come as friend, I come in peace,
   with love and respect for all that is here.
   Pray walk awhile beside me, open your world to me
   that I may come to know you better, as you share
   what you'd like me to see.'

4. Scatter some diced apples or organic seeds upon the ground as an offering of your goodwill.

Witchcraft Faith and Beliefs

Witchcraft faith and beliefs are focused on the Goddess and the Horned God, the two primary deities of witchcraft. They are sometimes referred to as the Mother Goddess and Father God or 'the Mighty Ones'.

These two deities have many subdivisions, with archetypes for every conceivable need from sea travel to childbirth. Their influences have no boundaries, and have been especially strong in Ancient Egypt, Greece, Rome, Northern Europe, India and the Middle East. This explains why certain witches work with Isis, while others worship Hecate and still others choose Cernunnos (a Celtic male deity) or Odin (from Nordic mythology). Although some may see these various forms as being different, they are ultimately aspects of the primary goddess and god whom all witches venerate.

Witchcraft is a tradition of respect and tolerance. This is demonstrated in the Wiccan Rede (Credo), see below. If you wish to live your life according to witchcraft values, it is important that you achieve a deep understanding of what the Wiccan Rede means. 'Perfect love and perfect trust' refers to our original state of innocence, in which our hearts are open and our feelings are receptive to divine will. The principle of harming none excludes us from, for example, gossiping, backbiting, negative thinking and hurting another's feelings intentionally. Living this way requires great integrity.

THE WICCAN REDE

'Bide the Wiccan law ye must, in perfect love and perfect trust.
Eight words the Wiccan rede fulfil;
an it harm none, do what ye will.
What ye send forth comes back to thee,
so ever mind the law of three.
Follow this with mind and heart.
Merry ye meet and merry ye part.'

For the Highest Good

When witches are initiated they take an oath to 'harm none' and to work for the 'highest good of all'. These are very deep and meaningful affirmations that aim to encourage practitioners to raise themselves above their lower human nature towards a more divine consciousness, that considers all life.

Working for the highest good of all challenges selfishness, egotism, jealousy, pettiness, ill will and many other limited human traits. When we are aligned to it rightly, it will wash our spirit with grace and blessings, although for this to happen, we must wholeheartedly dedicate ourselves to the highest good, with no expectation of anything in return.

Aligning with the Highest Good

Begin each day with a dedication to the highest good, using these words or those of your own choosing.

> *'May this day unfold to its highest good and may my thoughts, words and deeds be in alignment with the highest good of all.'*

When, or if, things don't seem to be going your way, turn your attention to the highest good and ask that all aligns and resolves itself rightly for the benefit of all. Consider how you can be of benefit to someone or something if it would be helpful and effective. Offer your time and/or presence where you feel called or drawn to help.

Dramas, outbursts and negative thinking are often not the most appropriate actions. As we move closer to a greater good these intensive atmospheres become less and less welcome as we move to a more enlightened state of consciousness. When something is rattling you or you can feel your emotions rising, try to step back, take a few moments to breathe deeply and do your best to align yourself to your highest potential.

We all carry the highest good within our being; it is the calm quiet voice that nudges us towards generosity of spirit and consideration of everything at those times when responses are called for. Our lower nature 'reacts', our higher nature 'responds'. Learning how to raise base emotions from charged reactions to measured responses is part of aligning with the highest good. A witch who is serious about their practice will strive to embody the highest good in all that they do.

Honouring the Goddess and the Horned God

Witches honour the Goddess and Horned God by working to embody the essence, or spirit, of these deities within their own being. This means that the goal for the female witch is to personify the Goddess, while the male endeavours to incorporate the qualities of the Horned God into his daily life.

In contrast to some other religions that teach about an afterlife where people will be rewarded in heaven or punished in hell, witchcraft brings spirituality firmly into the earthly domain, aiming for a mystical union between body and spirit. In witchcraft there is no separation between the spiritual and physical, there is no sin in the flesh. Because of this, witchcraft covens will often practise naked, or 'skyclad', as it is termed.

However, outside of coven practices, it is ultimately down to personal choice as to whether one goes skyclad or not. The important point is to honour and respect the human body and to consciously celebrate the gift that is life, body and spirit.

Meeting the Goddess and the Horned God

Witches recognize the Goddess and Horned God as being part of each of us, as well as being everywhere around us. We can meet them whenever we wish. As our spiritual Mother and Father, they will always give us guidance and love. In witchcraft, they are often personified as Mother Earth and Father Sky.

The purpose of meeting with the Goddess and the Horned God is to develop and build an intimate relationship with them as if they are loved family members and to realize that, as their children, we are always able to turn to them for spiritual comfort and support. Meeting them helps us to recognize that we are never alone.

The Goddess and Horned God are always with those who honour them; it is we who often ignore their presence. View the earth as the body of the Goddess and the sky and wildness of nature as the domain of the Horned God.

CONNECTING WITH MOTHER
EARTH AND FATHER SKY

1. Prepare a room (or in summer find a quiet place outdoors that attracts you).

2. Calm your inner self by breathing in to a slow count of four, pausing for a count of four, breathing out for a count of four and pausing again for a count of four. This is called the Fourfold Breath (*see page 55* – but please do not do this if you have a heart condition. Just breathe gently instead). Continue until you feel centred.

3. Let your spirit flow with love over the earth and then down into her through your feet. Draw her essence back up into your being through your feet, just as tree roots would.

4. Now, raise your arms towards the sky in a 'V' shape, palms facing inward, and let your spirit flow into the skies, the breeze and the sun. When you feel connected, slowly bring your arms down in front of you to waist height, a little out to your sides. Give your love to the trees, the creatures, the plants and the flowers. Then, with palms facing upward before you, imagine the love of the Horned God flowing toward you and filling your spirit with his love.

A MAGICAL OATH

A magical oath is your solemn promise to honour witchcraft values and is made to the Goddess and the Horned God. Witches frequently call the Goddess and the Horned God the 'Mighty Ones'. The oath is made to them through you and so you are making this promise to your higher self as well as to them.

The reason for taking the oath is twofold: to ensure that you are prepared to follow the witchcraft guidelines of harming none, and to raise yourself to your highest potential in thought, word and deed from that day on. The magical oath also affirms that you will not use the Craft in selfish ways.

TAKING A MAGICAL OATH

1. Create a magical atmosphere around your altar (*see pages 28–9*) with candles, incense and greenery (as well as appropriate music, if you like). Choose a special time, such as midnight or dawn.

2. Prepare yourself by bathing and then anointing yourself with sacred oil blended by putting five drops of frankincense into two teaspoons of carrier oil. Using your finger, anoint above your pubic bone as well as your feet, palms, breasts or chest, heart, throat and forehead.

3. Light your candles and stand facing the altar. Ring a bell to start. Then, visualize the Goddess and the Horned God standing before you, witnessing your oath.

4. Place one hand on your heart and the other before you, palm forward, and say the following:
   'I do solemnly swear in the presence of you Mighty Ones to honour the ancient way, to love the earth and respect all life. I pledge from this day on to work only for the highest good; to strive to harm none in thought, word or deed; and to extend myself beyond my human limitations to unite with you as my true self. I now welcome the sacred ways into my spirit. By your grace, the veil shall be lifted and I shall be deemed worthy of your ways.'

5. Bow your head and say:
   'My Lady, my Lord, witness this, my solemn oath.

6. Ring a bell to close.

GETTING STARTED
WITH WITCHCRAFT

'And round and round the circle spun
Until the gates swung wide ajar that bar the boundary of the earth
From fairy realms that shine afar.'

The Witches' Ballad, Doreen Valiente

To begin practising witchcraft, you will need to find figurines of the Goddess and the Horned God. These don't have to be expensive. You will also need to obtain the four witchcraft altar tools: the athame (a witch's sacred knife or dagger, used only in rituals), the wand, the chalice and the pentagram, which represent the four elements of air, fire, water and earth respectively. Witches lay out these tools on their altar during all ritual and ceremonial work because they represent the four elemental quarters of east, south, west and north in the circles that we cast. More details about the elemental tools can be found on page 24.

You must also consider where to cast your working circle, whether indoors or outside. For an altar, you can use any simple object, such as a small table, a chest or a box, or a natural object, such as a tree stump or a stone. Primary factors to consider are privacy, warmth, comfort and personal safety. Many witchcraft rituals are performed during the 'witching hour', which is around midnight. This is because all witchcraft practices aim to take the spirit beyond the activities of mundane daily life into moments less frequently visited. Periods such as dawn, dusk and midnight, when there is less 'human' activity and daily business going on to distract us, are ideal and, on a magical level, these times are each seen as a portal to other dimensions, too. However, this does not preclude you from performing rituals at any time of the day or night that suits you.

This chapter reveals how and when to cleanse, bless and consecrate items and areas prior to any magical work. Attention should be given to your magical equipment, robes, physical body and any special jewellery you may wear during rituals. Casting a working circle creates a place beyond ordinary space and time, where magic happens and the cares of the world can be left behind.

The Witch's Tools

The most significant tools a witch needs are the athame for air, the wand for fire, the chalice for water and the pentagram for earth. Witches also require candles and candleholders, icons of the Goddess and the Horned God, and two small containers for salt and spring water, plus a *Book of Shadows*. All of a witch's personal tools should have meaning. It is preferable to have a simple chalice received with love from a friend than a crystal chalice encrusted with jewels that holds no real personal meaning. Working tools can also be handmade, which many witches prefer, accepting gifts from nature for their magical equipment. The tools are:

THE ATHAME: This is the witch's sacred dagger, which traditionally has a black handle and a double-edged metal blade. It is important that this knife is not used for any purpose other than ritual work. A knife from your kitchen can become an athame as long as it is used only in rituals after its consecration.

THE WAND: This is a piece of wood up to about 46 centimetres (18 inches) long, which is handpicked from a live tree. This must be done respectfully and with awareness. Some witches and shamans have elaborate wands with crystals, feathers and magical inscriptions. It is a personal choice whether yours is plain or decorated, although traditionally wands are usually plain.

THE CHALICE: This is a cup or grail normally filled with mead, cider, wine or apple juice. It can be highly elaborate or delicate, or simply a wine glass that has been consecrated and then kept only for magical work.

THE PENTAGRAM: This is a circular piece of wood or metal with the five-pointed star either etched or painted within a circle upon it. It is normally placed in the centre of the altar between the two candles.

THE BOOK OF SHADOWS: This is the witch's personal sacred book in which rituals, spells, charms and documents are stored and referred to during magical work.

THE STAFF: Many witches have a personal staff. Some choose simple, straight staffs, others have shaped ones, and yet others prefer the 'Y'-shaped, forked stick, known as a 'stang', which represents the Horned God.

CONSECRATING YOUR MAGICAL TOOLS

Any items that you use for magical work should be cleansed, blessed, sanctified and activated for the highest good before use.

1. Lay out your altar (*see pages 28–9*) with your figurines of the Goddess and the Horned God and four representations of the elements as listed below:

   - a small bowl of salt for earth in the north
   - an incense stick for air in the east
   - a red candle for fire in the south
   - a small bowl of spring water for water in the west

2. Lay the items to be consecrated in the centre, over your pentagram if you wish. Light the incense and the candle and sit quietly for a few moments.

3. Take up an item and pass it through the incense smoke and say:
   'By the powers of air, may this [name the item] now be cleansed, blessed and sanctified for the highest good.'

   Pass it across the candle flame a few times and say:
   'By the powers of fire, may this [name the item] now be cleansed, blessed and sanctified for the highest good.'

   Now sprinkle it with a little water and say:
   'By the powers of water may this [name the item] now be cleansed, blessed and sanctified for the highest good.'

   Finally, sprinkle it with a little salt and say:
   'By the powers of earth may this [name the item] now be cleansed, blessed and sanctified for the highest good.'

4. Hold your item in both hands, face north and say:
   'By the powers of the Goddess and the Great Horned God, may this [name the item] now be blessed and sanctified for the highest good of all. So mote it be!' (this means 'So shall it be!')

Sacred Space

In witchcraft, all of creation is sacred. To us, the world is like a beautiful garden that was created by our Mother and Father for us, their children. In creating sacred space, we allow ourselves the time to feel the sacredness that is always present.

All environments, however, can be affected by pollutants (whether these are environmental or emotional). Therefore, the first step to creating sacred space is to cleanse the area. The next steps are to bless and invoke the sacred by visualizing light and love. Finally, we seal the area with a type of protection.

Witches create sacred space prior to all magical working, before setting up a magical circle, and when an environment seems to need cleansing due to daily stresses and strains. You can create sacred space anywhere and at any time in order to lift atmospheres or in preparation for your magical activities.

1. CLEANSING
Put three drops of rose geranium oil into a bowl of warmed spring water. Wash your hands, your face and your feet with it before you start. This will ensure that your energy is psychically cleansed. Enter the environment you have chosen (it can be indoors or outdoors) and face north. Light a sage smudge stick and hold it before you, letting the smoke billow in that direction. Visualize all pollutants leaving with the smoke. Turn east and do the same, but this time imagine that all cruel words and deeds are departing. Turn south and visualize all stale, old and tired energy being removed. Finally, turn west and imagine all pain and suffering being lifted. Turn north to complete your circle. Bury the lit end of your smudge stick in a bowl of earth to douse it.

2. BLESSING
Remain facing north and turn your palms toward it. Say the following blessing:
   'And it be for the highest good, may good now enter here and here remain.'

3. INVOKING
Stretch your right arm up toward the sky and extend your left arm down toward the earth. Concentrating upon your left arm, call to Mother Goddess as follows:
   'O sweet mother, giver of grace, I ask that you bless this place with your loving heart and hold it in your wise embrace. So mote it be!'

Focusing on your right arm, call to Father God as follows:
   Oh mighty one, Lord of all nature and guardian of this sacred Earth, I ask that you shield and secure this place with your protection. So mote it be!'

Imagine the energy of a beautiful mother rising through your arm and up to the heavens and the energy of a strong and reliable father descending through your other arm down into the earth. Stay in the experience for a few moments.

4. SEALING
Bring both arms to your heart and breathe with peace in your heart. Using the hand that you write with, draw a figure of eight (the witches' symbol of eternity, called a lemnascate) from north to centre in front of you, then east to centre, and so on until all four directions are completed.

5. Ring a bell to close.

THE WITCHCRAFT ALTAR

An altar is used in many spiritual traditions. In witchcraft, the ritual altar provides a focus for spiritual energy and is a place to put magical equipment during rituals and ceremonies. The witch's ritual altar is where we place the elemental tools, candles and other equipment that we may require during a ritual or magical event, so that we do not have to leave the sacred circle once it is cast. This ritual altar is erected just before casting the circle and is dismantled after completion. You can, however, display your magical tools on other altars around your home if you wish, or store them away.

You should set up your witchcraft ritual altar just before your magical event. It can include an altar cloth, although this is not compulsory. Your altar should be large enough to hold your equipment. A small, portable table or chest would be ideal. It is usually placed in the north, east or centre of the circle, depending upon your preference and practicality.

ARRANGING YOUR ALTAR

1. Cover your table with an altar cloth, if desired, and set two candles on either side at the back. Many witches use black candles, as in witchcraft black is the colour of peace, tranquillity, deep spirituality and meditation. Consider your ritual to determine which colour candle best suits your focus or intent (*see pages 56–9*). Place your pentagram plate in the centre of the table. Then put the chalice, which you have filled with apple juice, red wine or cider on the platter.

2. Place small icons of the Goddess and the Horned God on either side of the pentagram, and your athame at the side. Place your wand on the other side of the pentagram. (*See* Witchcraft Tools, *page 24*). Position a small container of spring water and a small bowl of salt on either side of your pentagram plate. Keep a saucer nearby for your libations. (A libation is a fluid offering made to the Goddess and the Horned God from the chalice after the circle is cast but before you begin your actual ritual. First, you pour your offering to the Goddess and then to the Horned God, after which you take a sip yourself.)

3. Arrange any other ritual items, such as your bell, incense burner and *Book of Shadows*, where there is space. You can also include other decorative items that in some way reflect your ritual or magical intent – for example some fallen leaves in autumn, a small Yule log in winter, bulbs in a small pot in spring or a brightly-painted sun icon in summer.

4. When the altar is set up, light the candles and incense and sound the bell. Then kneel in front of it for a few moments in meditation, consecrating it in your mind to the four elemental guardians and dedicating it to the highest good, which is always under the guidance and protection of the Goddess and Horned God. You are now ready to begin your magical work. Ring the bell, extinguish the candles and leave the area in preparation for entering again to start your ritual event or celebration.

THE SACRED CIRCLE

In witchcraft, a sacred circle is used to define the special area in which formal ritual working is to be performed. The circle is not a barrier; it is a doorway to another world, a magical and mystical place where the conditions and rules are different from the everyday world. The circle is also a container for your magical energy and any magical power that is raised, preventing it from dissipating until it is used. The sacred circle is not a two-dimensional circle marked on the ground, it is three-dimensional, more like a globe; it is a spiritual energy that is visualized in the mind.

You can cast a sacred circle for all magical acts. Its size should comfortably contain those using it. You will need to perform certain actions and speak certain words aloud in a clear voice. You should place your witchcraft altar in the north, centre or east of the circle.

CASTING YOUR CIRCLE

1. Prepare yourself by bathing, and clear and cleanse your chosen area. Set up your altar.

2. Light your altar candles. Take your athame from the altar and walk clockwise around your circle, visualizing a globe appearing as you do so, saying:
   'With this sacred blade I cast the circle of our Craft. May it be a doorway to that sacred circle that is beyond space and time. Let it be a meeting place for all good and may it repel all weakness.'

3. Stand before your altar, pick up your bell and say:
   'In the names of the Goddess and the great Horned God, I cast this my/our working circle.'

   Ring your bell.

4. Return to the north, raise your blade high before you and call out:
   'Bear witness, spirits of the north, ye guardians of witchcraft.'

   Go to the east, south and west and repeat appropriately.

5. At the altar, put your salt bowl on the pentagram and lower the point of your athame into the bowl of salt, saying:

   'I exorcise thee, oh creature of salt, that thou be purified and thus may aid me well.'

   Put your water on the pentagram and take a pinch of salt and sprinkle it into the bowl of water. Lower the point of your athame into the water, saying:

   'I cleanse and consecrate thee, Water of Life, that thou mayest bless this circle. In the names of the Goddess and the Horned God, so mote it be!'

6. Take up the consecrated water and go slowly round the circle again (still clockwise), sprinkling a few drops along the line of the circle, saying:

   'I consecrate this sacred circle by the powers of earth, air, fire and water. May the Goddess bestow her love herein and the Horned God his honour.'

   Take up your chalice, pour a small amount in the saucer for the Goddess and Horned God as a libation and then take a sip yourself. After you have done this, place the chalice behind or back on your pentagram.

Your circle is now cast and you can perform your specific activity here, such as a Sabbat ritual, making a charm or healing. Complete your chosen work and then move on to closing your circle.

CLOSING YOUR CIRCLE

1. Go to the north, hold up your blade and say:

   'Guardians and spirits of the [north] wind, this ritual is now done. I/We bid you hail and farewell. Hail and farewell.'

   Repeat counterclockwise from north to west, to south, to east and back to the north again.

2. Extinguish your altar candles and bow your head at the altar, saying:

   'I declare this sacred circle dissolved. So mote it be.'

Ring a bell to complete the closing and step out.

The Witch's Calendar

*'Hoof and horn, hoof and horn, all that dies shall be reborn
Corn and grain, corn and grain, all that falls shall rise again.'*

Traditional Witchcraft chant, Ian Corrigan

The witchcraft calendar is also referred to as the Wheel of the Year. This Wheel represents a full cycle of the seasons of spring, summer, autumn and winter. Each season brings certain gifts. In spring, it's new life, youth, potential and the stirring of the seeds. In summer, it's warmth, light and the vibrancy of nature growing. In autumn, it's the harvest and the fruits of our labours. In winter, it's rest, introspection and renewal. Each season is marked by a series of festivals to honour the particular qualities of that time of year. Witches help to turn the wheel of the seasons through both acknowledgement and enactment of each seasonal focus through their rituals.

The witchcraft calendar includes four Greater Sabbats and four Lesser Sabbats. The four Greater Sabbats of Imbolc, Beltaine, Lughnasadh and Samhain are also called the four agricultural festivals and are very ancient pagan rites. The four Lesser Sabbats are the spring (Ostara) and autumn (Mabon) equinoxes and the winter (Yule) and summer (Litha) solstices, which are later additions to the witchcraft calendar. These Lesser Sabbats acknowledge distinctions between the forces of dark and light throughout the year and fires or light are often significant.

By enacting what should occur as each season rises and falls, witches empathically connect with the powers of creation and effectively try to mirror what is happening in nature. For example, at Imbolc when the maiden Goddess returns to herald the birth of spring, witches may invite a coven member dressed as a maiden in a veil and white robes into their homes. This way they literally welcome in the spring.

An Introduction to the Festivals

The Greater Sabbats are highly spiritual occasions, undertaken with greatest regard and dignity. In all witchcraft rituals and ceremonies the sanctity and sacredness of the occasion is always honoured and respected. Because these rituals are meant to embody the powers of creation, they should be considered to be serious occasions. This does not mean that laughter, celebration and joy are not present. These aspects are most often invited after the cakes and ale are introduced at the end of the ceremony. Sometimes there is direction written specifically into the ritual event, for example, witches may be asked to dance and sing. Understanding the meaning of each festival allows witches to write their own rituals that incorporate the flavour of each festival within their words.

The Greater Sabbats

Samhain
Colours: orange, black, white
Samhain (pronounced 'sow-en') begins on the eve of 1 November (31 October) and marks the end of the Celtic year. Because this night is neither old nor new, it stands at the threshold between. It is therefore associated with the ancestors and the Otherworld. Samhain is the time when witches honour the ancestors and perform divination.

Imbolc
Colours: white, pastels
Imbolc (pronounced 'imolk') begins on the eve of 2 February (1 February) and marks the first spring fertility festival with the return of the maiden Goddess to the earth as she brings in the dawning of spring. Witches make candlelit processions to sacred wells and springs, cleanse and bless local waterways and invite the maiden (spring) into their homes.

Beltaine
Colours: green, gold, red, white
Beltaine (pronounced 'beall-te-nye') begins on the eve of May (30 April) and is one of the most magical witchcraft festivals. It is the third fertility festival on the Wheel. It is associated with fairies, magic and love. Anything magical and romantic is welcomed. Many couples get handfasted (married) at this festival, and those ending a relationship may perform a hand-parting at this time.

LUGHNASADH

Colours: orange, ochre, brown

Lughnasadh (pronounced 'loo-nah-sah') begins on the eve of 1 August (31 July) and is the first of the three witchcraft harvest festivals. It honours the declining powers of the solar warrior-god Lugh and gives thanks for the harvest about to be gathered. It is also a time to make an appeal for good weather until the crops are safely harvested. Traditionally, bread is made and mead is brought to make offerings to the Goddess and the Horned God to symbolize our thanks for their bounty.

THE LESSER SABBATS

The four solar festivals or Lesser Sabbats occur at Yule around 21 December (the winter solstice), Ostara, on or around 21 March (around the spring equinox), Litha around 21 June (the summer solstice) and Mabon around 21 September (the autumn equinox). Being fire or solar festivals, all light is usually extinguished before new fires or beacons are lit to mark the turning of the Wheel.

YULE ALTAR: red and gold; evergreens, vanilla, pine, cypress, mistletoe

OSTARA ALTAR: white and green; white cone lilies, seeds, grains, eggs

LITHA ALTAR: red and green; the staff, roses, elderflower, meadowsweet, vervain

MABON ALTAR: rich autumn colours in all hues; cornucopia, green man, stag, cider, acorns, bread

Working with the Wheel of the Year

Since the Wheel of the Year symbolizes the turning of the seasons, you can have seasonal altars and plan seasonal activities and rituals that complement each time of year (*see also page 94*). Choose a place in your home that you can adjust as the seasons change. For example, you can collect feathers, stones, moss, leaves, flowers and fruits to arrange on your seasonal altar. This helps you to make a deep connection to the turning of the year.

It can be very helpful to keep a journal to record observations about your journey through the year. Linking with the natural world in this personal way will heighten your observances of when, for example, the first snowdrops appear or the hawthorn blossoms emerge. You can note bird migrations, flight patterns, dawn choruses and anything else you like. You can walk through the twilight and perhaps encounter a badger on country lanes or receive a blessing from a swooping bat. Keeping records in a journal helps you connect to nature. You begin to know when to expect certain flora and fauna and at what time of day, night or year they are most active. This way you will know, for example, roughly when you could gather meadowsweet or elderflowers, crab apples or acorns. It is very helpful to develop your own guide for which season you should gather your herbs, fruits or nuts for magical work. It is always best to make your lotions, oils or concoctions during the season when your ingredients are active. For example, a holly essence is best made around Yule time, whereas rose-petal water is best made in the warmer months.

Experience what each season feels like within your own being. As winter approaches, most of us begin to withdraw from social activity. But with the promise of light, in contrast, we emerge and become much more active. This is a very simple example of how the seasons can affect us. We can have more profound experiences by standing at midnight on frosted grass during the winter solstice, performing a magical salutation to the sun at dawn, or gathering the dew on Beltaine morn, which is said to be the gift of true love's nectar from the Fairy King and Queen.

Build your confidence in performing the Greater Sabbat rituals that honour each season and then reach out to find your own ways of expressing each time of year, through ritual, poetry, storytelling, craftworking or perhaps singing and drumming.

The great joy of witchcraft is that it celebrates as well as venerates the natural world. Human beings are part of nature and so any way that we, the children of the earth, wish to honour our spiritual Mother and Father is seen as an act of love toward them, as long as we remain sincere about it. Be confident in yourself and know there is no such thing as a mistake in witchcraft when we are doing our best to act from the perspectives of love and respect. Experiment, explore, enjoy and emulate these witchcraft ideals and, by the grace of the Goddess, you will be shown her magic.

The Rhythms of the Moon

The moon is intimately associated with the triple Goddess of maiden (new), mother (full) and crone (waning/dark). She holds deep occult secrets and is the revealer, the reflector, the inner guide. The moon is associated with magic, healing, fertility, conception, nature, water, women, dreams, psychism and the weather. Her day of the week is Monday and her most potent time is at full moon.

Lunar timing plays an integral part in magical work, because witches believe that each weekday, each hour, each season and each time of day has a distinct 'flavour' to it, which can be incorporated into the fabric of any magical work.

Each phase of the moon carries certain powers: new to full is for attraction; the full moon is manifestation of desires and wishes; and the waning to dark is for release. To call for a new beginning, choose a waxing moon. For endings, release or removal, choose a waning moon.

By referring to the chart opposite, you can make your own lunar charm bags, spells and healing amulets simply by combining different ingredients.

The new moon is associated with Artemis and Thoth, and assists with conception of a variety of ideas, plans and projects, including pregnancy. It can help other things in your life to grow as well. Seek the new moon to attract things to you.

The full moon, associated with Isis, Diana, Aradia and Arianrhod, is powerful and should be approached with respect and reverence. Seek the full moon when you wish to manifest something in your life on a physical or practical level, such as a child.

The waning moon is ruled by Hecate, Cybele and Cerridwen. It is the time when things can be cast away and released. It is also the time for banishings. The waning moon allows us to withdraw and to move forward. Time is given for reflection and release of that which is as yet unmanifested.

The dark moon is the one night when no moon is seen in the sky. Like the waning moon, it is governed by the dark goddesses, who are also referred to as the wisdom keepers. It is, therefore, the best time to focus your efforts upon meditation and you can gain insights through contemplation of your inner world. Chaos can abound at this time because this is also the night of the Norse valkyries and the Irish banshees, spirits that both herald death.

THE LUNAR PHASES

NEW: Attraction   Potential, forward planning, new growth, conception

FULL: Manifestation   Magic, wishes, dreams and desires

WANING/DARK: Release   Letting go, healing, psychic development, banishing, envisioning

THE LUNAR CORRESPONDENCES

DAY OF THE WEEK	Monday
COLOURS	White (new), silver, red (full), light blue (waning), black (banishings and dark moon)
MINERAL	Silver
CRYSTALS	Pearl, moonstone, clear quartz, shells, water and river stones
DIRECTION	West
ELEMENT	Water
NUMBERS	3, 9 and 13
TREES	Willow, aspen, eucalyptus, pear, driftwood
FLOWERS	Jasmine, camellia, lotus, lilies, camphor, sandalwood, freshwater and ocean plants, reeds, poppy, night-scented blooms, watercress and all white flowers
AROMA	Coconut, sandalwood, eucalyptus, camphor
ANIMALS	Hare, hound, wolf, bat, fox, bear, cat, owl, toad, frog, lioness, serpent, snail
MYTHICAL CREATURES	Unicorn, moonhare
DAY OF THE WEEK	Monday
DEITIES	Artemis, Nimue, Cybele, Diana, Isis, Arianrhod, Selene, Arcadia, Hecate, Nanna, Thoth, Cerridwen, Lilith
ELEMENTAL SPIRITS	Undines, for emotional maturity and developed perceptions.
SIGIL OF THE MOON	

Lunar Esbats

Esbats provide opportunities for meetings either as an individual or as a coven throughout the year for teaching, healing and education beyond the more ceremonial and religious tones of the Sabbats. An esbat is usually fixed to fall on, or around, a full moon or a new moon, and so can provide the opportunity for up to thirteen meetings each year (or about one a month). A focus for each meeting is planned in advance (such as understanding runes, personal responsibility or earth healing). Any subject that pertains to wisdom is appropriate. Attendees then contribute whatever they can to the event or simply come to learn by absorbing the teachings. A few days before the esbat, consider what teachings your evening will focus upon and gather books, magazine articles or perhaps even invite a friend who is knowledgeable in your chosen subject.

Healing is offered to those who have asked for it. If the event is a coven esbat, questions are answered by the high priestess or priest. There is also a period of reflection or meditation.

The Goddess or the Horned God are honoured in some way, usually with cakes and ale – edible and drinkable offerings that have been blessed before ingestion.

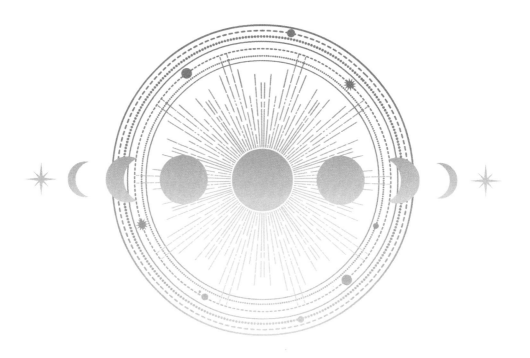

DRAWING DOWN THE MOON

Prepare your selected area to make it magical and create a special mood with candles, lanterns, crystals, flowers, greenery, magical icons and anything else that inspires you. Place a circular mirror (available from hardware stores) in a bowl of spring water on your altar to represent the moon. Place a clear quartz crystal on the mirror.

1. Open your circle and then dedicate the evening to the Queen of Heaven – the moon. Light three white votive candles in your moon bowl and say:
   'Blessed Light of Night, I honour you,
   Mother Moon.'

2. Perform the Triple Goddess Salutation in three movements as follows:

   Stand with your arms cupped upward at your shoulders in a 'U' shape. Bring your arms up over your head with each hand in a 'C' shape and then cross your wrists, with your hands still making a 'C' shape outward. Keeping your wrists crossed, bring them down to your heart. Then, bring your arms down toward the ground and sweep each palm outward, face downward, over the earth beneath you.

3. Meditate for about five minutes upon the light and qualities of the moon descending into your moon bowl, focusing your love and healing thoughts into the bowl as well.

4. Pour some of this water into your chalice. After offering some to the Goddess's libation bowl, take a sip of the moon water yourself. You can put some of this moon water in a bottle and offer it as a drink to anyone who has asked for healing.

5. Extinguish your votive candles and thank Mother Moon.

You can then carry on with the evening's chosen teaching subject, if part of your event, before closing the circle.

Greater Sabbat Rituals

Samhain

The festival of remembering the ancestors, Samhain, marks the end of the Celtic year and the dawning of the new year. It honours the last of the harvest festivals for the year just passing. The crops are in and the days become ever shorter and darker. Since this night (31 October) rests on the threshold between the old and new year, it is considered to reside between the worlds. Thus, the veils that separate spirit from matter are thinner and more easily crossed than at other times of year. This is an ideal night for divination, as well as for remembrance.

A RITUAL FOR SAMHAIN

1. Set up your witchcraft altar with black and orange colours, black candles, a bell and a white pillar candle. Add a skull or bones, pictures of departed loved ones, a jack-o'-lantern (carved pumpkin) and any divination tools you have, such as tarot cards, a crystal ball or runes.

2. Light two black candles and open your circle in the usual way.

3. Go back to your altar, light your white pillar candle, ring your bell ceremoniously and say:
   'Light of spirit, I bid you welcome. Come to the circle
   to bless all souls departed.'

   Sit in contemplation for at least five minutes, recalling memories of your loved ones, of the ancestors you never knew, and of your origins at the dawn of human life. Consider your lineage and what might have happened before you existed. Then, give thanks back through time to all of your relations whose unions meant that you now have life. Ring the bell again when you feel you have completed this. You can sit, kneel or stand before your altar during this activity. If you are performing divination, begin that now or go to Step 5.

4. Take up your divination tool(s) and walk to all four quarters of the circle. Stop at each one saying:
   'Guardians of the north, [east, south, west], open may the
   doorway be to the mystic realms beyond this mortal shore.
   Grant this night the eyes of one that sees, 'tis time to read the
   signs you bring once more!'

   Then, perform your divination.

5. Give thanks for your guidance and say
   'Light of spirit, may souls in conflict rise in peace with you,
   may all those lost find their way home to you and may
   your blessings be upon us all. Fare thee well.'

   Extinguish your pillar candle. You can now close your sacred circle as usual. Make sure you ring a bell to mark the closing, which will ensure that all spirits have departed.

Imbolc

Imbolc, the dawn of spring, begins on the eve of 2 February. Traditionally, candlelit processions gather at sacred wells and springs. We bless the waters that give us life and welcome in the maiden. She who gave birth to the new sun king at the winter solstice is now ready to turn the Wheel to another season. At Imbolc, she is the virgin bride returning to the earth to prepare herself for her Lord's seed, which will provide the harvest in the coming year. Imbolc (meaning 'in the womb' in Gaelic) represents the stirrings of new life.

Set up your witchcraft altar with white and pastel colours and a small bowl of almonds. The shape of the almonds symbolically represents the vagina or divine entrance to the womb of life. Spring flowers, especially snowdrops, can be included as long as they are not picked from the wild. Place a corn dolly or a small figurative doll, dressed in white, on the altar in a little cradle-shaped container filled with hay, wheat or corn stalks. Craft a small wand for the doll and leave it in the cradle. Then, put sweet offerings beside the cradle in a bowl. Draw the vesica symbol, below, onto some small pieces of paper and place them on your altar – you will need these for the ritual.

A RITUAL FOR IMBOLC

1. Do not light your two altar candles yet, but open the circle as usual in every other respect.

2. Dedicate your Imbolc ritual to the virgin Goddess by saying:
   'Babe in the cradle
   Maid at the door
   Gifts from the goddess
   awaken once more
   in the seed and the
   grain and the gentle
   spring rain.'

   Knock on something to imitate a knock at the door. If there is more than one person present at this ritual, a person dressed in white can actually knock at a closed door that another person can open saying, 'A welcome fair maid, come in, now, come in.' Lead your spring maiden from the door to the altar or, if on your own, sweep your hands from the direction of your front door toward the babe on the altar.

3. Light your two altar candles now and sit quietly for a few moments. Consider the light of spring returning to the earth to warm the ground and prepare it for the planting. Each person present now takes an almond kernel and, holding it in their hand, contemplates the gifts of new life that the maiden brings. Place the almond(s) in the cradle. Add the gifts from your offering bowl that you have either made or bought especially for the spring maiden (such as violets, snowdrops, little rosewater biscuits or seashells), sending love to the babe as you place them in the cradle.

4. Write a wish for something(s) you would like to manifest or birth in your own life in the central portion(s) of the vesica symbol of fertility, which you drew onto snippets of paper earlier. Take up the maiden's wand and tap it three times over your wish(es) and then lay the paper gently in the cradle.

Close your circle, but leave the babe and the cradle on the altar overnight. In the morning, gather up all the grasses and offerings (including the wishes) and bury them together in some fertile soil.

Beltaine

Beltaine, a most magical festival and the third of the spring fertility celebrations on the Wheel of the Year, begins at sunset on 30 April – the day before 1 May. The meadows and trees are green and vibrant, filled with life and vitality. The nature spirits sparkle everywhere in joyful celebration of the return of their floral and leafy dwellings. Now is the time to celebrate the magic, to call for new relationships, for joy, for fertility, for the blessing of unions with a handfasting and for the acknowledging of relationship endings with a hand-parting.

It is traditional for couples to jump the Beltaine fire together, especially if they wish to conceive.

If weather permits, perform this ritual in the woods or meadows. You will need a stick that is painted with red and white stripes and hung with red and white ribbons and bells (topped with an optional pine cone). You also need a small bowl of sesame or sunflower seeds. Display hawthorn sprigs, violets or pansies and wear ivy tendrils. Burn candles in lanterns hung from the trees. Traditional folk music and drumming make good accompaniments.

A RITUAL FOR BELTAINE

1. Set up a natural altar, such a flat-topped stone, bedecked with greenery. Place on it your decorated wand, a chalice filled with water and oatcakes (or other unprocessed plain grain crackers, such as water biscuits or digestive (graham) crackers). If possible, prepare wood and kindling so you can light a small bonfire for the ritual, if fire is allowed and no damage could be caused. Open your circle.

2. Dedicate your ritual to the Goddess and the Green Man by saying:
   > *'Lady of the Hills and Meadows, Lord of Nature's mantle green*
   > *We gather on the eve of May to bless our Sacred King and Queen*
   > *Whose fertile seeds ...'*

   Cast your seeds upon and around the altar.
   > *'... and tender rain ...'*

   Take up the chalice and walk in a circle around the stone, flicking it with water.
   > *'... unite as lovers once again.'*

   Pick up your decorated wand and turn it between your palms so that the ribbons swirl and the bells tinkle, saying:
   > *'Hearken, for their sighs of love do whisper through the greening grove.'*

3. Take up your drum, rattle, penny whistle or musical instrument and play and dance in a spiral motion away from and toward the stone altar in the middle, giving your energy to the earth and to the union of the Goddess and the Green Man. You can play taped music if you prefer. Once your spiral dance is completed, you can light your bonfire. Throw oatcakes into the flames, dedicating each one to appease any wrathful gods and feed the pleasure of the kindly ones. You can also throw in oatcakes for Bel (a sun god associated with Beltaine) and the Lady and Lord.

4. Collect ash from the Beltaine fire once it is cooled and keep it for fertility rituals and protection from harm. Traditionally, animals were also led through the ashes with invocations to protect them. As soon as the fire is safe to jump, you can leap across if you wish.

LUGHNASADH

The first of three witchcraft harvest festivals, Lughnasadh begins on the eve of 1 August. Named after the warrior sun god, Lugh, it is the time for taking oaths, signing contracts, showing feats of strength, playing games and celebrating. Appeals to Lugh were for good weather until the harvest was safely home.

As with Beltaine, Lughnasadh is a traditional time for unions; it falls nine months before Beltaine. Since only couples with a child could 'marry' in ancient days, it is likely that couples who joined together at Lughnasadh and were still childless by Beltaine would perform a hand-parting rather than a handfasting.

For this ritual, you will need berries from the hedgerows and trees, bread or small cakes, some corn or wheat stalks, and some apples and nuts.

A RITUAL FOR LUGHNASADH

1. Set up your altar with the fruits, corn, nuts, apples, bread and berries. Also include orange altar candles, approximately 46 centimetres (18 inches) of orange cord, some ochre and brown colours, and a circular plate of harvest crops. You should place your chalice in the centre, containing either mead, cider or apple juice, with eight unlit votive candles arranged around it. Open your circle.

2. Dedicate your ritual to the harvest and to Lord Lugh and the Grain Mother by saying:
   'Here do we gather together in joy, as we prepare to bring in the harvest of the year just lived.'

   Take up the bread/cakes/berries and say:
   'We give thanks to our Grain Mother for her wondrous bounty.'

   Break the bread or offering over the harvest plate. Everyone participating says:
   'Hail and welcome Lady.' Share a morsel each.

Then say,
> 'Lord Lugh we bid you a hearty welcome at our feast.'

Raise the chalice and pour a small amount of fluid over the harvest plate. Take a sip yourself and then pass the chalice around to any others present. All say,
> 'Hail and welcome, Lord.'

3. Light the eight votive candles and say:
    > 'The sun wheel turns and turns again,
    > Light, bright on fields of grain.
    > Harvest now the seeds we've sown
    > In colours of the Mother grown.
    > Now we gather what we reap.'

    Take up your ears of corn or grain and say:
    > 'Weep not Grain Mother, for pending sleep
    > shall bring you rest and comfort deep.
    > We shall hold you until spring
    > and you return to weave and spin
    > new life in the seed and grain.
    > Weep not Grain Mother, as your
    > Sun Lord wanes,
    > for the wheel it turns and turns again.'

    Bind the stalks with orange cord and keep this harvest bundle on an altar until the spring. It represents a home for the Grain Mother during the winter months.

4. Consider the passing year and be thankful for your life. Consider, too, what has not come to pass and let it go. You can make commitments to a partner and make promises of things you will try to achieve. Close your circle.

Then, take your harvest offerings outside for the wildlife. Play games and be joyful.

WITCHCRAFT AS A PATH TO SELF-DEVELOPMENT

'The Veil of Isis sevenfold, to he as gauze shall be
Wherethrough clear eyed he shall behold the ancient Mystery.'

The Voices of the Soul, V.J. Daley

All witches take an oath at their first degree that marks their initiation into the Craft. They vow to harm none, to live in perfect love and perfect trust, to work on developing themselves to a greater understanding of their true nature and to act unselfishly for the benefit of all. With these promises in place, the witch begins the journey of a lifetime. It is the most wondrous journey, because they are working to uncover their own true nature. Solitary witches can still approach some covens to ask for initiation as a witch without obligation to join a coven.

In witchcraft, self-development does not happen through grabbing power and prestige, nor is it gained by 'looking the part'. It is achieved through dedication and devotion to the seeking of wisdom, love and awareness. The magic is only revealed to those who are willing to grow. The way of the witch opens you to the most profound understandings that can only ever be experienced personally. Witchcraft is predominantly an oral tradition for this reason; it cannot ever be an intellectual exercise. Unless you have prepared yourself and advanced in your spiritual integrity, you will not have the experiences. Magic is everywhere – in the stones, the stars, the streams and the seasons. Just for a moment, contemplate the fact that you are on a small rock that is hurtling through space, en route to the edges of eternity. Is creation not the most incredible mystery to you? Learning to resonate with these universal truths within our own spirit is part of the magic. This chapter will help you to begin to raise your awareness toward those magical realms that you hold within your soul.

The Three Degrees of Advancement

Within the coven system of witchcraft there are three degrees of advancement. The first degree is bestowed on an individual at the point of initiation as a witch to mark them joining the Craft. At this stage the initiate is called a priest or a priestess. Advancement in personal and spiritual understanding prepares the initiate for the second degree. When they feel ready, they ask for this initiation. Second-degree witches are called high priests and high priestesses and at this stage a female can start her own coven. The third degree is the most difficult to attain and is considered the degree of perfection as a witch. Third-degree witches will not reveal their grade publicly. All three degrees require personal effort, dedication and spiritual attainment.

Only those with true courage can succeed in progressing successfully through the three degrees. It is only by working on ourselves and by striving for wisdom, love and truth that we can develop. A vital part of witchcraft, therefore, is self-development. The exercise that follows will help you to open to your greater self and free your spirit from the limitations of the mundane world.

A SELF-DEVELOPMENT MEDITATION

Always have a candle lit during this exercise, which represents the illumined Spirit. It invites the presence of the powers of transformation that are held within the fire element. This exercise is best performed in the morning because of its energizing qualities. It is a powerful meditation, so you should allow at least ten minutes after you finish to readjust back to everyday consciousness.

1. Light frankincense incense and let the smoke waft around you and your space. If you like, gently breathe in the incense. Perform the Fourfold Breath (*see page 55*) for a few minutes. Remain standing.

2. Visualize a star of purest light high above your head. From this star radiates a beam of whitest light. It descends in a column of brightness, sparkling with flecks of tiny silver and gold particles, going through the top of your head, down toward the earth and around your body. Feel the column of light passing down through you and all around you.

3. Feel the light touching any shadows, blocks and tensions within your body, allowing them to be replaced by the sparkling light as it descends slowly through you. Imagine that the shadows are being gently pushed out through openings in the soles of your feet and down into the earth.

4. When your body and spirit feel cleansed, rejuvenated and filled with light, close the openings in your feet. Let your whole body be filled and encircled with light for a few minutes. Once you are filled, let the column of light return back up to the star and on an out breath, slowly open your eyes.

Breathing Techniques

For thousands of years, many traditions have considered the breath to be a doorway to the mysteries. Witchcraft also respects the breath as a magical tool. By understanding and working consciously with the breath, we can raise our awareness, release stress, balance our energy and connect to our spirit. Some witches have the ability to raise the wind or heal through chanting into wounds. Both are air element gifts and our breathing is the physical connection to it. We can only survive without air for a few moments. It is our most vital connection to the forces that give us life.

You can use these breathing techniques to calm yourself, release fears and anxieties, prepare yourself for magical work and connect to your spirit.

PEACE BREATHING

Peace breathing can be used when you wish to calm stresses and emotions and when you wish to release something.

1. Find a warm and comfortable spot. Either lie down with a pillow beneath your head or choose a suitable straight-backed chair, where your feet can easily touch the floor. Turn off your phone and ensure that you will not be disturbed for at least fifteen minutes.

2. Set a timer for fifteen minutes. Place it beneath a cushion so it will not startle you when it rings. Lie down or arrange yourself in your chosen chair.

3. Place your hands on your stomach. As you breathe in, attempt to push your hands out as if you were blowing up a balloon in your stomach and pushing your belly out. This ensures that you are breathing deeply. Breathe in as far as you can, but do not hold your breath. Imagine that you are inhaling peace throughout your body.

4. Keeping your hands on your stomach, heave a big sigh. Exhale as completely as you can until you cannot breathe out any more air. On this out-breath, visualize that you are releasing all tension, stress, emotion or anxiety. Relax your muscles with each exhalation and simply let the in breath come when it does. Continue until the alarm rings.

5. Upon completion, stretch your limbs. Then, open your eyes on an out-breath. Turn on one side and get up very slowly from the floor, or rise from the chair carefully.

THE FOURFOLD BREATH

You can use this breath to raise your awareness and to prepare for all magical work, however please don't do this practice if you have heart problems or a pacemaker. As mentioned on page 19, the Fourfold Breath is a magical breathing technique.

1. Find a comfortable spot sitting or lying down, where you will not be disturbed for about five minutes.

2. Breathe in to the count of four, hold your breath for the count of four, breathe out to the count of four and then hold your breath for the count of four. Find a way to balance the timing of your breathing by repeating something (such as 'one manitou', 'two manitou' and so on. (A manitou is a supernatural life force that, according to Algonquian belief, pervades the natural world.)

UNDERSTANDING MAGICAL CORRESPONDENCES

Correspondences provide a means to focus the ingredients for your magic in a particular direction. By the way you put them together, you can achieve a desired result. The easiest way to start is to decide which day of the week best suits your magical work. Then, refer to the chart (*see pages 58–9*) to see what else you could include to complement and support your intent. Correspondences strengthen the intent, thus making it clearer for the magical realms to receive and interpret. Grasping correspondences takes time and effort, but is a necessary and vital part of ritual and magical work.

The chart overleaf gives you a sample of correspondences that will allow you to perform effective magic. Plan to perform your magic on the day of the week that best fits the magic you are going to undertake (such as Friday for love, Monday for healing, or Sunday for success). Then, look along the table to see which fragrances, herbs, crystals and deities you could work with to support your magical request. You will also notice that colours are part of the table. For example, you could use a purple cloth and purple candles when working with Jupiter on a Thursday. This table has just a handful of correspondences to get you started.

It is important not to manipulate reality for selfish reasons. Always precede your magical work with the saying, 'An it be for the highest good and by Divine will...' (this is an archaic way of saying 'If it be for the greater good...') This will indicate that you are content to accept whatever outcome is best, or the one that is part of your true destiny.

— • ☾ ✳   APPEALING TO A DEITY   ✳ ☽ • —

1. Set up an altar with the appropriate correspondences chosen in accordance with the chart overleaf. Open your circle in the usual way.

2. Drum, rattle or dance around your circle to raise your energy. Then, perform the Fourfold Breath (*see page 55*) for a few minutes. Do not do this breath if you have heart problems or a pacemaker.

3. Repeat the following request three times while facing your altar:
    '*Lady/Lord...* [state your name here], *this night/day I beseech thee, come to this Circle and hear my plea for...* [state the full reason for your magic, such as healing or love]. *This I pledge for highest good – hear me Lady/Lord – so mote it be!*'

4. Ring a bell and close your circle.

CHART OF MAGICAL CORRESPONDENCES

DAY OF WEEK	MONDAY	TUESDAY	WEDNESDAY
PLANET	Moon	Mars	Mercury
GOVERNS	fertility, dreams, revelations, healing, psychism, emotion	conflict, power, protection	travel, study, communication
COLOUR	white (new moon), silver/red (full moon), pale blue (waning moon), black (dark moon)	red	yellow
GEM/CRYSTAL	clear quartz, pearl, moonstone	ruby, hematite	agate, carnelian
SYMBOL/SIGIL	♄	~	♀
HERBS	camphor, sandalwood,	coriander, tobacco, garlic	caraway, marjoram
FRAGRANCE	jasmine	pine	lavender
DEITIES	Diana, Isis, Selene, Hecate, Cerridwen	Woden, Ares, Thor	Thoth, Mercury, Athena

THURSDAY	FRIDAY	SATURDAY	SUNDAY
Jupiter	Venus	Saturn	Sun
luck, law, fortune	love, friendship, relationships	obstacles, timing, land, inheritance, karma	prosperity, success, health
purple, turquoise	green, pink	black, indigo	orange, gold
turquoise, amethyst	rose quartz, emerald, jade	jet, obsidian	amber, sunstone
nutmeg, cinquefoil	myrtle, violet	evergreens, asafoetida	bay leaves, mistletoe, marigold
honeysuckle, cloves	rose	cypress	frankincense
Juno, Hera, Zeus	Branwen, Aphrodite, Venus	Herne, Cronos	Lugh, Sekhmet

Magical Charms

Originating from a Latin word (*carmen*) meaning 'song', charms are magically-charged occult articles made by, or for, the wearer to avert negativity or to invite good luck. Our modern-day charm bracelet originated from this practice. Charms can be made with any ingredients as long as the magical correspondences and items we use are associated with the charm's intended purpose. A love-attracting charm would need to include ingredients associated with love (such as the colours green and pink), the goddess Aphrodite and herbs and spices associated with love, such as myrtle, rose or basil. Refer to the magical correspondences chart above on pages 58–9 for more details.

LOVE CHARMS

In order to fully understand how to make effective magical charms (and, in fact, for any witchcraft magical practices), you will need to explore and understand correspondences. Investigate reference books on correspondences and build up the confidence to put things together that are associated with your focus. All herbs with links to love can be included in a love charm. This can be done by weaving them in, anointing the object with its fragrance or oil, or burning herbal incense associated with love as you weave your love web. Appropriate love crystals, tree berries, spices, associated love icons, symbols and signs can all be included. Imagination and creativity are all part of magic. There is no set way to create magical charms. Each is unique to the maker and to the needs of the wearer. Once you have your ingredients, plan your making to coincide with the next full moon.

MAKING A LOVE CHARM

1. Find a willow tree in your vicinity. When the moon is full, carefully and respectfully remove a 46-centimetre (18-inch) young tree branch. Don't forget to give your thanks to the tree. Soak the branch in warm water to make it flexible, if necessary.

2. Bend the branch into a hoop and fasten the ends firmly together. Weave thin green cord or thread around and through your hoop to create a web effect. It does not have to look like a work of art.

3. Quietly keep repeating the following love chant under your breath:
   'Here I weave a web this night, filled with love and
   warmth and light,
   Come to me my lover true, let me share love's joy with you.'

4. Continue to weave and bind the ingredients that you have gathered into your threads to complement and strengthen your charm's powers – for example, three, seven or nine basil leaves, paper roses, heart shapes, crescent moons and ivy tendrils – until your charm feels suitably completed. You can also hang swan, dove or duck feathers from your charm if you like, because they are birds traditionally associated with love.

5. Hang your charm above your bed and, every night, repeat your wish for true love to find you. When fulfilled, go to the willow tree from which you cut the branch. Bury your charm beneath it and give Mother Willow your thanks.

WITCHCRAFT SERVICE TO OTHERS

Witches see all human beings as potential brothers or sisters. We are all children of the Goddess and the Horned God and therefore equals in their eyes. Anyone wishing to follow witchcraft ideals will therefore practise kindness, compassion, tolerance and respect for everyone, regardless of any incompatibility or differences. Authentic witches live by the ethics of integrity, honour, truth and love, as much as they are able.

Witchcraft service to others can be shared on many levels, the main criteria being to care. If there is a need and we are able to help in any way, then witches offer their services appropriately. At no time will witches interfere or take over a situation. They will simply offer support and help where asked.

PROTECTION WITHIN A SACRED CIRCLE

This magical act can be performed for others who ask for your help, or for yourself, should you find you need extra protection or strength. As with all magic, the first thing you must do is to decide which is the best day of the week to weave it. For protection, the best planet to work with is Mars. Your altar, tools and accessories should all reflect Martian powers. This means red candles, as well as offerings of dynamic fiery spices and herbs, such as garlic cloves, black peppercorns, tobacco and chillies, laid out in an offering bowl.

1. Set up your altar to your chosen planet on a Tuesday (the day of Mars). Cast your circle in the usual way.

2. Go back to your altar, take up your wand and walk around the circle. If you don't have a wand, walk around the circle with an altar candle. As you do so, say:
   'By the powers of fire, a ring of fire I make, to guard from harm, the good they do forsake. Ring of fire keeps me [or state the name of the person requiring protection here] *safe, ring of fire keeps me safe, ring of fire keeps me safe. So mote it be!'*

3. Put your wand back on the altar. Sit, kneel or stand before your altar and visualize a circle of red, orange and gold flames all around you until you feel and genuinely believe that they are strong and vibrant all around you.

4. Pick up your offering bowl and visualize the ring of fire around you being drawn into your spices, activating their magical properties and filling them with protection and power. Once you feel that the flames have all moved into your spices, pack them into a little pouch or bag and give them to the person in need or carry them with you, as and when you need them. Keep them close by for as long as needs be. When no longer needed, bury the pouch beneath a holly or a pine tree, or a gorse bush, with your thanks.

5. Close your circle in the usual way.

THE NATURAL WORLD

'Earth my body, water my blood
Air my breath and fire my spirit.'

Traditional witchcraft chant

How extraordinary it is that all our needs are met by the natural world. We have been given our food, water, shelter, warmth, building and craft materials, clothing and leisure possibilities. It is even more awesome when we take into account our human gifts of music, dance and creativity. We really are truly blessed to have this planet as our home.

So many of us have lost that vital connection to the earth, to the simpler pleasures such as watching a sunset, a moonrise or a shooting star. So few of us consider how lucky we are to have food and water. We often fail to appreciate our life until it changes in some way to our detriment.

This chapter explains the deep connection that witchcraft has with the natural world and describes ways to begin working more sacredly with it. We explore the four spiritual elements, the nature spirits, the changing seasons and frameworks for the seasonal festivals in the four Greater Sabbats. The spiritual elements are distinct from the chemical elements in that they are the spiritual quality of each element. With spiritual water, for example, we are relating to water's emotive, feeling nature and not to the physicalities of flowing water or rain. The nature spirits are elemental essences from the natural world and exist as nature's unseen or energetic presences that we can honour and work with cooperatively in order to be shown the magic of nature. Witchcraft is natural. It is nature, fertility and the harvest. Explore the festivals in this chapter and find the qualities of your true nature emerging as a result.

Sacred Ecology

Sacred ecology means caring for the earth and all of her creations in a wider context than solely conservation or sustainability alone. Witches recognize the spiritual beauty of life on Earth and work consciously to honour and respect all life forms, whether they be a tree, an animal, a flower or an insect. Witches can be termed sacred ecologists because they strive to be guardians of the planet and see all of its kingdoms as a sacred human responsibility. The human race is destroying the ecology of the earth rapidly and thoughtlessly. Witches, however, work to love and preserve the earth, not to destroy her, because she is our spiritual Mother.

If you wish to emulate these witchcraft ideals, strive to conserve the resources where you live. Care for the earth and keep it well-loved. Join local conservation projects, recycle, compost as much as you can, and educate yourself about global conservation and wildlife preservation projects which you could make a contribution to. Get active! Taking personal responsibility is vital. Many people ignore problems until they are right on their doorstep. Unfortunately, with regard to preserving endangered life on this planet, that will simply be too late. We must act now and act swiftly. Here is what you can do to help:

CUT CONSUMERISM: Look at each room in your home and minimize trash, clutter and any unnecessary items. Make the minimum of purchases that you actually need for your household. Decorate your home with 'green' paints, environmentally-friendly furniture and 'fair-trade' products (items that have been bought fairly from developing countries, without exploitation). Cut down your consumerism wherever you can. Repair and reuse wherever possible.

GROW YOUR OWN: Build a compost bin and recycle all compostable waste for reuse on your garden. Grow your own vegetables and herbs without chemicals where you can.

GO ORGANIC: Buy organic and eco-friendly products available from all good natural/organic product outlets. Join a local organic produce scheme, where you have organic vegetables delivered to your door once a week. Buy healthy items from local farmers' markets. Support local initiatives that conserve the planet's resources. Eat and live wisely.

GET ACTIVE: Join conservation organizations, educate yourself about global issues and refuse to support companies that damage the environment. Support environmentally-friendly projects and don't use products that pollute or damage our world. Lobby local parliament or government representatives to support environmentally-friendly initiatives. Let your voice be heard.

OFFER PRAYERS: The power of prayer can be used in areas where there is a need for love and caring, but you are unable to make a physical contribution – such as a war-torn country and places around the world suffering famine or drought.

CONTEMPLATION

Light an emerald green candle and quietly sit in daily five-minute contemplations, focusing on your chosen area. Send peace, love and your caring thoughts into the candle flame and imagine that all darkness and suffering is being lifted and loved away. Stay calm and repeat regularly throughout your contemplations:

'An it be for highest good, may the gift of [state the requirement here, like 'water', 'food', 'peace'] *find those who suffer this day. Mother, Father, please aid your children as I shall aid them however I am able. Hear this plea, I beseech thee.'*

Mother Earth

Witchcraft today, perhaps more than at any other time in history, can help humanity to return to its roots in nature. The precepts of 'the highest good' and 'harming none', when practised rightly and with deep respect, encourage practitioners to be of service to creation and to help where possible. The Earth doesn't need healing, she needs humanity to stop destroying her. When each and every human being can live to the best of their ability, without harming, our Earth will be safe. To me, this is why witchcraft can play a significant part in humanity's very necessary journey back to more conscious and compassionate living.

Along with practical involvements, such as making lifestyle changes to exclude anything that has the potential to be harmful to life, witches will be very aware that there is also an energetic realm – a place where intention is formed and alignments can be forged. In days of old, there was a 'blessing witch' – someone who had the ability to create powerful prayers and invocations. Being a blessing witch today and wishing all life well will ultimately return to us a deep sense of wellbeing and, by adhering to such practices, we will also be doing our best to be aligned to the highest good.

AN EARTH BLESSING

Intention can be a powerful thing. At those times when we cannot be directly involved, cannot take helpful action of some kind, we can perform an earth blessing ritual.

1. First of all, prepare yourself and your surroundings so that all is peaceful, sweet-smelling and calm.

2. Turn off phones and shut out distractions.

3. Decorate a low table or area with a circlet of flowers and place a crystal or glass bowl in the centre. Float a night light in the glass or crystal bowl that is three-quarters filled with spring water.

4. Light your night light and then sit before your altar and ring a bell or gong to begin.

5. Visualize the Earth slowly and gently spinning and turning in front of you and floating suspended and roughly at eye level with your forehead or brow about 30 centimetres (12 inches) above the bowl beneath. Around this Earth imagine a bubble made of crystal-clear, pure light that is enfolding the planet in serenity and peace. This crystal light is healing and calming.

6. Hold the Earth in this bubble of light, visualizing our planet at peace, and that humanity is in harmony with all life that lives upon it. Feel for peace within yourself, feel for peace for all life, open your heart to send your love and healing swathed in this pure light around the globe. Imagine life on this Earth being warm and happy, joyful and rich, and a safe place to call home. Believe in peace and goodness, hold to brightness and right outcomes for all.

7. Upon completion of your visualization, you may wish to say something like:
   'Peace and light enfold the Earth,
   Thus all life is touched with love.'

8. Extinguish your night-light. Ring your bell or gong three times to complete. You can do this visualization as often as you like.

A WISHING BUNDLE TO MOTHER EARTH

As well as wishing blessings for the Earth, at those times when we feel the need, we can also ask for her assistance or guidance by creating a wishing bundle.

For a wishing bundle to Mother Earth you will need the following items, but please ensure that all contents are biodegradable, natural and preferably organic.

- 12 bay leaves
- Thin thread, to bind
- Cotton for making bay leaf fans
- 41-cm (16-in) square piece of white material, such as muslin or cheesecloth
- A seashell
- A red flower
- A cross (this can be two twigs bound together)
- Rice
- Tokens that represent your needs or request
- Thicker thread, to bind
- Anything you feel drawn to put in as your own offerings: sweets, leaves, acorns, twigs etc.
- Images of your wish or words of your wish on natural paper

1. Take three bay leaves and bind them with the cotton, using the thin thread, to make a fan shape. Do this four times, so that you end up with four small bay leaf fans.

2. Place the white cloth on a flat surface. Place the seashell in the centre and the cross upon or in it. Lay the fans around the shell. Either put a whole red flower on or in your design or break off the petals and sprinkle them around.

3. Now build up a beautiful picture on your white cloth, so that it looks enticing, rich, tasty and a suitable offering to give to Mother Earth. Be generous, but do not put in anything that would pollute or poison her – natural, biodegradable and preferably organic things only .

4. Once your offering is made, take up the four corners and gently pull them together. Bind these with the thicker thread and then bind all over the bundle with the thread to hold it secure and keep its parcel shape.

5. Meditate with the bundle in your hands, visualizing your wish or need, and then ask the Mother to guide you to the place it should be buried. Bear in mind that this can be anywhere, so is not always necessarily somewhere convenient, such as your garden... so be open. She will not suggest somewhere unrealistic.

6. Ceremoniously bury your bundle and don't dig it up again. Give your thanks and let the Mother grow answers to your prayer.

Exploring the Four Spiritual Elements

The four elements of earth, air, fire and water are manifested in physical reality by solidity, fresh air, winds, warmth and light, rain, oceans, rivers and lakes. These are physical aspects of each element. The four elements also have qualities in the spiritual dimensions that can be used to develop a deeper spiritual and personal understanding of our true nature, because we embody the spiritual qualities of each element as well as their physical aspects.

AIR

The physical air element is closest to spirit (or ether), which is the space that contains all of the spiritual and physical elements. When Spirit descends into the physical elements, it travels from Spirit into air, air into fire, fire into water and water into earth, travelling from the most refined down to the densest. Thus, to bring Spirit down to earth, we begin with the air element and the qualities of spiritual air.

Within the air we breathe we can also find the qualities of spiritual air, those finer virtues so lacking in the human spirit these days – honesty, integrity and honour. In magic, the air element is considered masculine.

Negative Spiritual Air
The unrefined manifestations of spiritual air include negative thinking, poor communication skills, gossip, inability to learn and grow, tyranny, fear and anxiety, dishonesty, mental chaos and psychic confusion.

Positive Spiritual Air
The pure qualities of spiritual air are honesty, the ability to learn and understand, integrity, clear communication, constructive thinking, honour, mental harmony, clairaudience (hearing Spirit) and intellectual brightness.

EXPLORING THE SPIRITUAL AIR ELEMENT

1. Set up your altar in the east of your circle – the direction for the air element. Lay it out in yellow and lilac colours, with yellow candles, your athame, agates, amethysts and/or turquoise crystals, hazel fronds, violets and lavender flowers, a Thoth statue or picture. Burn lavender incense and lay your athame on the altar between the candles.

2. Light your altar candles and then cast your circle. Kneel or sit before your altar, holding your athame toward it and invoke mighty Thoth (te-ho-te), an Ancient Egyptian deity whose teachings were associated with air:

    'Mighty Thoth – with you I breathe the spirit of air into my being. Teach me, Lord, the ways of truth, honour and understanding. Breathe your wisdom into me and help me embody my greater self.'

3. Draw a large upward-facing 'A'-shaped triangle with your athame in the air before you, with a line across its centre, and visualize Thoth (the ibis-headed deity) standing at the other side of the triangle, as if it were a doorway. Breathe in through the triangle, imagining the purest qualities of spiritual air filling your lungs and body. Breathe out any impurities or lower spiritual-air attributes you feel you have back through the triangle toward Thoth. Honesty with yourself is vital at this point. Continue for at least five minutes.

4. Give thanks to Thoth for his presence and pledge that you will strive to be honourable from that point on. Close your circle.

FIRE

The physical aspects of the fire element are warmth and light. The fire of the sun is central to creation for, without it, there would be no life. The spiritual essence of the fire element does not consist of the physical flames we see with the naked eye, rather it is a vital energetic and vibrant force that brings courage, strength and valour. Spiritual fire is transformative – moving the seeker to greater consciousness by 'burning away' those things that no longer serve them well. In terms of masculine and feminine, the fire element represents the masculine, and in magic is considered an active rather than a passive force.

Spiritual fire, as when making a real fire, requires a sacrifice of some kind: with the tree, it is its branches; with the candle flame, its waxen body. With humans, for example, cowardice must be sacrificed for bravery to emerge.

NEGATIVE SPIRITUAL FIRE
When it is met by lower frequencies in the soul, spiritual fire can produce aggression, domination, cowardice, temper, erratic behaviour, unpredictability and egotism.

POSITIVE SPIRITUAL FIRE
The purest qualities of spiritual fire are courage, valour, inner conviction, joy, strength, humility, compassion, humour, passion and transformation.

EXPLORING THE SPIRITUAL FIRE ELEMENT

1. Set up your altar in the south of your circle and lay out your altar to the fire element. Include reds, oranges and/or golds in your colour scheme, with two orange altar candles, one pillar candle in gold, marigolds, your wand, oak leaves, cloves, and orange crystals like carnelians and amber. Burn cedar incense or frankincense. Also, have nearby, a fireproof container, matches and small pieces of paper and a pen. You can display lions, phoenixes and salamanders as well.

2. Light your altar candles and cast your circle. Light your gold pillar candle and take it and stand in the south of your circle facing outward. Hold out your candle and say:
    'Here do I call for the spirit of fire to illuminate my being.
    Lords of the spiritual Sun, come hither to lighten my shadows
    and brighten my soul. In you I entrust my spirit.'

3. Take your pillar candle back to your altar and place it in the centre. Sit before your altar and consider carefully and deeply what you need to sacrifice in order to transform yourself into your greater self. Write on a piece of paper a single fire-based word that sums up what you will give to the spiritual essence of fire via the candle flame, such as anger or egotism.

4. Before casting your pieces of paper into the golden candle flame, gather up as much of the particular limitation from inside yourself as you can and visualize giving it to the fire. Once lit, drop the paper into your heatproof container and leave it to burn to ashes completely. Give thanks to the sun lords and close your circle in the usual way.

WATER

The physical water element flows across most of the Earth and our bodies contain over seventy-five percent of it. We birth in physical form from the waters of a womb. The spiritual water element presides over the emotions, the feelings and perceptions. It is flowing by nature and teaches us how to be flexible and adaptable. Just as physical water cleanses, quenches and cultivates the land, so spiritual water brings us opportunities to cleanse emotions, quench our spiritual thirst and cultivate our inner being with love. The water element represents the feminine, and in magical work is considered a passive rather than an active force.

The water element also governs sleep, dreams, psychism and relationships of all kinds.

NEGATIVE SPIRITUAL WATER
Spiritual water, when hindered by blocks in the soul, induces over-emotionalism, reactionary behaviour, stagnation, insecurity, doubt, inflexibility, depression and mood swings.

POSITIVE SPIRITUAL WATER
The purest expression of spiritual water is love, flexibility, adaptability, cooperation, clarity, developed intuition, serenity and grace.

EXPLORING THE SPIRITUAL WATER ELEMENT

The spiritual water element helps us to develop clear boundaries, clarity of purpose and direction and understanding of our inner feelings.

1. Lay out your altar in the west of your circle to the water element with blue, silver and white colours and two blue candles. Add a bowl of water in the centre containing water habitat flowers, such as a lily or iris, your chalice, jasmine flowers, icons of water creatures like dolphins, otters, whales or seahorses, and clear quartz crystals, moonstones or shells. Moon icons are also appropriate, as are an indoor fountain and an Isis statue. You can also put on some calming, rhythmical music, if you wish.

2. Cast your circle and light your altar candles. Standing facing your altar, pick up your chalice (which you have filled with spring water – ideally, from a sacred well) and invoke the Lady Isis to come and join you by saying:
   'Blessed Lady of Grace, I stand before you as your child. Help me to understand the sacred ways that flow from you unto my heart. Cleanse my spirit Lady, let love touch my soul and heal its sorrows. So mote it be!'

3. Put your chalice back on your altar, place your hands across your chest over your heart and close your eyes. Meditate in this position upon your inner feelings, fears, doubts and insecurities. Let tears flow if they come, for tears are the language of the heart. Contemplate whatever troubles you. Continue this for at least five minutes. Uncross your arms and cup them upward at shoulder height and ask Lady Isis to lift any such troubled feelings or other emotions away from you and out into the chalice. Open your eyes and gaze upon the water flower and consider its beauty, for you, too, carry that beauty in your soul.

4. Give thanks to Lady Isis for her presence, close your circle in the usual way and take your chalice water to tip into a lake or river.

EARTH

The earth element provides us with the material world, with all matter, food, vegetation and species. These are the physical aspects of the earth element. Spiritual earth invites us to wisdom and understanding, to make connections and realize our place in creation and to honour and respect the earth, to being reliable, to embody all the best attributes of a Mother Goddess, full of unconditional love. The earth element is defined as feminine and, in magical terms, is considered passive.

As with all things we have the choice whether we move in negative or positive ways with earth's spiritual potential.

NEGATIVE SPIRITUAL EARTH

The base, more negative translation of spiritual earth energy within our characters includes obstinacy, stubbornness, sexual dysfunction, insecurity, inflexibility, belligerence, unreliability, meanness, laziness and sloth.

POSITIVE SPIRITUAL EARTH

The highest qualities of spiritual earth would include wisdom, stability, reliability, protection and strength in adversity, self-defence, endurance, clairsentience (sensing/feeling spirit), nourishment and abundance. Witches work with the earth element when needing to protect someone psychically, because of its abilities to earth and stabilize unwanted or overcharged energy.

EXPLORING THE SPIRITUAL EARTH ELEMENT

1. Set up your altar in the north, with earth element correspondences of green or black candles, a bowl of clean earth, fossils, ferns, root vegetables and any black or green stones or crystals you may have. Burn cypress oil in an aromatherapy burner on your altar as well.

2. Light your candles and then cast your circle. Take a pinch of earth into the palm of each hand. Holding the essence of the earth, make the following invocation to Gaia, the Earth Mother:

   'Mother, I come to remember the spirit of earth within my being. I ask that you guide me to its wisdom, to the spiritual teachings held within your sacred earth. So mote it be!'

3. Consider your character carefully and be totally honest with yourself about who you feel you really are and how you behave in life.

   Allow the essence of the earth that you hold in the palms of your hands to enter into your being and guide you to places within yourself that hold spiritual earth. Focus on areas you know you could improve – for example, perhaps you know you are a little unreliable. Allow the spirit of earth's higher qualities to energetically move any negative earth qualities you have into the physical earth that you hold in your hands. Feel that space being replaced by the dignity of spiritual earth. When you are finished, place the earth back in the bowl.

4. Pledge that you will strive to raise yourself to a greater good within your spiritual being, give thanks to Gaia for her presence and close your circle. Take your bowl of earth outside and respectfully sprinkle it over the ground, visualizing whatever negative earth you placed in the physical earth being transmuted into food for new life.

Nature and the Elementals

Elemental Spirits

Witches believe that all physical elements have spiritual counterparts that are presided over by their elemental spirits. For air, it is the sylphs; for fire, it is the salamanders; for water, it is the undines; and for earth, it is the gnomes. These are the spirits of the four elements.

Creating an Elementals' Nature Garden

If you have a garden, you can honour the elemental spirits there. For the sylphs, include bells, chimes and things that move in the breeze in the east of your garden. For the salamanders, include lanterns, votive candles, fairy lights and things that reflect rays of sunlight (such as metal disks) in the south of your garden. For the undines, include water fountains, ponds, decorative shells, clear crystals and water plants in the west of your garden. And for the gnomes, include mosses and lichens, wild plants and flowers, herbs, fallen tree bark, rocks, stones and fossils in the north of your garden. If you do not have a garden, create a magical area in your home by miniaturizing these suggestions and arranging them on a tray or in a large shallow bowl. Regularly tend it and love it to show the elementals you care.

Invoking the Elemental Spirits

Stand facing the elemental direction you wish to invoke and adapt the following version in each case:

'I stand to honour you [sylphs], *spirits of* [air]. *Bless the breath of life* [air], *light* [fire], *love* [water], *wisdom* [earth] *that you bring. May our spirits fly* [air], *shine* [fire], *flow* [water], *walk* [earth] *together always. So mote it be!'*

Nature Spirits

Nature Spirits are slightly different from elemental spirits in that they are specific to trees, plants, herbs and flowers rather than the four elements of air, fire, water and earth. The dryads are tree spirits and the devas are flower spirits, all held within the embrace of our Mother and Father, the Goddess and the Horned God.

TREES

In days of old, trees were highly venerated. Pagans would perform ceremonies in tree-clad groves and meet within circles of trees, called 'tree cathedrals' and witches particularly would gather in stands of hawthorn trees. Westminster Abbey is built upon a place that was once called Thorney Island – in recognition of the thorn trees that once stood there. During the suppression of witchcraft many superstitions were generated around certain trees to make them too dangerous to be associated with – all done in attempts to quash our ancestors' pagan practices and worship of nature.

WITCHES' TREES

- The elder
- The blackthorn
- The hawthorn

All trees can be approached for healing, through their particular qualities of energy in spirits known as dryads, with each tree providing a different kind of strength or ability that you can attune yourself to at times when, perhaps, life is getting you down or you are seeking help with a health problem or a personal issue. The practice of touching wood comes from a time when tree spirits were be invoked by touching certain woods – for example, for luck or protection (*see page 83*).

THORN TREES

Thorn trees deserve a special mention because of their close links to magic and witchcraft.

Solitary hawthorns are considered 'fairy trees' and to cut or damage one will incur their wrath. Sit beneath or beside a solitary hawthorn to journey to the realm of the Fae and the Otherworld, once you have gained permission from the tree, of course! You can also draw upon the magic of oak, ash and thorn as places where the Fae dwell, by twining twigs of these trees together and holding them when journeying to the Otherworld.

In folklore, the blackthorn was known as the 'cursing tree' and was used for dark magic; however, it is also highly protective against such intentions. A witch's staff would often be made from blackthorn wood for this very reason.

All thorn trees are protective because of their spines, which can be used to provide psychic barriers. However, blackthorn cuts should immediately be treated medically, as they can easily go septic.

Honouring the Trees

If you would like to connect more closely to the trees, adopt one in your local area and take care of it; build a relationship with it. You can then ask for its guidance or support, request healing or whatever you need in return, marking the event with perhaps a whispered wish wrapped inside one of its leaves.

As with all times when a witch works with nature, you should develop a symbiotic relationship where there is give as well as take, where there is gratitude and appreciation and an awareness that whatever you are working with is sentient and must be treated with respect. Nature sees us!

CONNECTING WITH THE DRYADS

Centre and calm yourself with some deep breathing. Sense your connection with the tree dryad, then sit with your back leaning against the trunk and close your eyes. Now visualize a door in the trunk of the tree. Knock three times upon the door and see it open. You are greeted by a tree spirit who you ask to let you in. Enter only if you are invited inside. You look around this new environment and take in the scenery. You can now ask the dryad to take you on a journey to find a healing solution or personal guidance, or even for some support and friendship, if the spirit is prepared to cooperate.

In your mind's eye, journey together wherever the dryad takes you – perhaps down a tunnel or through a maze of roots and rocks – whatever happens, trust the dryad and go with them. If you remain by the entrance, this is also fine. Spend as much time as you need and then return to the door. Bid your farewells, give your thanks and step back through into your everyday world. Open your eyes.

You can, if you like, leave a strand of your hair, a crystal or another little organic gift for the dryad by your tree, to show your appreciation.

TOUCHWOODS

ALDER	Patience
APPLE	Goodwill, love
ASH	Insight
ASPEN	Endurance
BEECH	Learning, mental clarity
BIRCH	Cleansing, clearing
BLACKTHORN	Averting evil, negativity; a 'Witch's Tree'
ELDER	Spell or hex breaking; a 'Witch's Tree'
ELM	Connection to nature spirits or elves
HAWTHORN	Connecting to the Fae; love; the 'Hedgewitch's Tree'
HAZEL	Wisdom
HOLLY	Fertility, protection
OAK	Luck, courage
ROWAN	Protection
WILLOW	Emotional support
YEW	Spiritual purification

Herbs and Flowers

Magical herbs, along with many other natural resources, are part of what is called the doctrine of signatures. These are basically correspondences of similarities that provide a focus for intention, helping to create the right environmental vibrations for the chosen intent.

When working with herb-lore, look at the folk names of your plants, which can often give indications as to how they were used in the past. For example, woodbine (honeysuckle), which comes from 'wood' and 'bind', is a binding plant that attaches itself well to trees and other natural anchor points. Therefore, it would be excellent for binding spells, too.

HERB	FOLK NAME	PLANET	DEITY	USAGE
Angelica	Archangel	Sun	Venus	protection, banishing
Basil	Witch's herb	Mars	Krishna	prosperity
Bluebell	Fairy flower	Moon	Selene	toxic – handle with care; binding spells, love
Brambles	Bumble kites	Venus	Brighid	Protection, prosperity
Cinnamon	Sweet wood	Sun	Ra	passion
Cypress	Tree of death	Saturn	Cronos	release, wisdom
Dragon's blood	Zanzibar drop	Mars	Horus	energy
Frankincense	Olibanum	Sun	Ra	consecration
Garlic	Poor man's treacle	Mars	Hecate	healing, protection
Gorse	Broom	Sun	Lugh	love, fertility
High John root	Jalap	Saturn	Kali	removes opposition
Honeysuckle	Woodbine	Jupiter	The Dagda	love, luck, prosperity
Ladies' mantle	Lion's Foot	Venus	Bast	dew brings life changes
Lily of the valley	May Lily	Mercury	Queen of Elphame	counters spells, attracts faery
Meadowsweet	Queen of the meadow	Jupiter	Juno	love, harmony
Mugwort	Artemesia	Venus	Artemis	clairvoyance
Mullein	Hag's tapers	Mercury/Saturn	Zeus, the Dagda	healing, safety, astral travel
Myrrh	Mu-Yao	Sun	Isis	purification
Myrtle	Bayberry	Venus	Astarte	love, fertility
Poppy	Blind eyes	Moon	Ceres, Hecate	sleep and dreams
Rose	Love flower	Venus	Aphrodite	love, beauty, peace
Rosemary	Dew of the sea	Venus	Aphrodite	memory, purification
Rue	Herb of grace	Sun	Aradia	health, healing
St John's wort	Hypericum	Sun	Sekhmet	exorcism, lift the spirits
Thyme	Bitter mint	Venus	The Faerie	relieves nightmares, health, magic
Vervain	Enchanter's plant	Venus	Cerridwen	love, inspiration, magic
Willow	Witches' aspirin	Moon	Selene	wishes
Yarrow	Blood wort	Venus	Isis	divination, protection

Nature Spirits

Many human beings in the West today have lost their vital connection to nature and the natural world to the point where they no longer feel part of it, or in any way reliant upon it. This is not the case. Without nature we cease to exist. Learn to honour what supports and nourishes you and take time to respect, preserve and enhance all life on Earth. Meeting with nature spirits enables human beings to become more attuned to nature and to the planet that sustains us.

MEETING NATURE SPIRITS

1. Choose to meet either a dryad or a deva (flower spirit) by selecting your tree or flower first. This can be absolutely any that you feel drawn to.

2. Settle yourself and your energy before approaching your chosen flora and announcing your presence and intention. Place a little gift or offering, such as a piece of your hair, a small crystal or some dried fruit by your flora. Then, if you have chosen a dryad, say:

   'Dryad of this sacred tree, I ask you now reveal to me, the hallowed place in which you dwell, how may I learn to know you well?'

   Or, if you have selected a deva, say:

   'Deva of this blessed flower, gentle spirit come to me now to teach my heart the sacred way, and live in beauty every day.'

   Touch the tree trunk carefully or cup your hands gently around your flower and close your eyes. Breathe peacefully and without expectation for a while.

3. A nature spirit should appear in your thoughts if you are quiet and peaceful enough. They will talk with you mentally, guide you and answer any questions you may have. If your heart is in the right place, the spirits will always honour you with their presence.

Respecting the Natural World

If we wish the secrets of nature to be revealed to us, we must be prepared to give something of ourselves, such as our time and energy. Too often in life we take without giving and showing gratitude, and this includes our attitudes to nature. Mother Nature is finite. Without our sincerity, care and respect, she will never reveal her magic, nor touch us with her grace.

COMMUNING WITH SPIRITS OF PLACE

Every environment and habitat has their spirit of place or guardian, whether indoors or outside. Here is how you can begin to be respectful of habitats and seek connection with them.

1. Take yourself to a place of your choice in nature and breathe in the air, feel the earth beneath your feet and speak your intent to the local spirit:
    'Spirit of Place, Guardian Spirit, I come in peace.'

    Knock your staff on the ground three times and then say:
    'Grant me entrance to your domain.'

    Wait awhile for your answer and focus on your surroundings – perhaps the leaves rustle, a robin or other bird flies by, the sun breaks out from clouds or maybe even a shadow passes.

2. Move with dignity and deference in that habitat, open your mind to the mysteries hidden there and let yourself be led and guided by the Guardian Spirit through its domain. There may well be a gift of a feather, a seedpod or a rare plant waiting for you to commune with. (Please don't pick endangered species.) Be open and trusting of the Guardian Spirit.

3. When you are ready to leave the chosen place, turn to face where you have been, bow your head and say:
    'Guardian Spirit, your honour is mine honour. Thank you for guiding me through. Now I must leave you. Farewell.'

SEEKING ANSWERS FROM NATURE

All creatures, birds and insects live in the domain of nature as well as trees, crops and vegetation. We can learn so much by simply being with her, for we too are part of the natural world. When we are coming from the right place within ourselves, Mother Nature will send messengers to answer questions and ease a troubled mind.

1. Formulate your question clearly and concisely in your mind and feelings. Take yourself and your staff outside to somewhere you feel safe and secure. Hilltops and sacred circles or sites are ideal.

2. Draw a clockwise circle above your head with your staff and invoke the Mother Goddess and the Father Horned God thus:
    'In the names of the Goddess and Great Horned God,
    I cast this sphere upon the winds.
    Come heed my call I beseech thee,
    help me, guide me, teach me.'

3. Wait and watch, for somewhere something will come to you – perhaps a bird or an insect. Or your eyes will be drawn to a small flower in the grass, or maybe a passing creature rustling nearby, or cloud formations in the sky. Let your spirit receive its message, and trust that your intuition will understand the answer if you are patient and open to it. There are many reference books that give meanings to the messages of birds, creatures and plants, if you need to refer to words.

Nature Cures

A nature cure can be as simple as walking barefoot on the grass and feeling the earth beneath our feet at those times when we simply need some 'breathing space', or as complex as treatments with potent plant derivatives for more severe health concerns.

To me, a nature cure is something else, too. It can also be finding and understanding the nature of something in order to respond to it appropriately. I believe that to learn the nature of things on as many levels as possible is also an important part of becoming a more conscious human being – a truly magical practitioner.

Everything has its own nature, its signature. This forms the basis for sympathetic magic and magical correspondences. Once something's nature has been identified, we can act accordingly and, with correct attitudes and approaches, bring all back to its rightful place.

You must have the appropriate qualifications these days to administer medicines internally or to diagnose or treat any conditions for anyone or anything beyond day-to-day ailments in family members and/or pets. Being aware of this and of the need to take appropriate medical advice when necessary, it has been my experience that magical healing methods (and thus nature cures) greatly suit the treatment of psychological or spiritual levels of dis-ease; the emotional and sub-conscious levels that are sometimes difficult to name and/or tame; the breaking of habits; and the development of self-understanding and, therefore, of self-love. They are also good for any psychic disturbances or upsets and also facilitate investigation into the root causes of things when there are obstacles, patterns or phobic fears. In addition, nature cures can help to clear the mind, ease sleep and improve concentration or confidence.

It is said that whatever ailment exists, whether it is spiritual, mental, emotional or physical, there is a cure for it and so it becomes a question of knowing where and how to find that cure. I know I am not the only witch or pagan who turns to nature in my quests to discover the most appropriate healing path. By finding the nature of the unrest, we can find the way to its peace.

I believe it is important to study the nature of the ailment/animal/client on as many levels as possible, through such things as developed perceptions, intuition, feelings, insights, and any relevant previous experience, through meditation, ritual and healing intent. This way can also include looking for the root or cause of something through psychic dialogue, in order to discover the nature and origin of the ailment or issue. At a shamanic level, if guided to, we can commune with it in order to understand it and thus know how best to work effectively to heal or help it. And at a physical level we can have dialogue with the client, and with various affected parts of the body where appropriate.

Mother Nature – the wisest and most wondrous teacher of all – is where we can freely go to commune with the nature spirits, the elementals, the creatures, colours and tones of our earth, and observe the patterns of the natural world, read the signs while feeling the 'energetics' of the situation or ailment, utilizing any developed skills and magical abilities to ascertain what the most effective and right approach or involvement might be. We can achieve this in several ways, such as through path-working, journeying, communing, psychism, divination or the exploration and study of folklore, and so on. Being able to stand in both this physical world and the Otherworld – without preference to either – is a vital part of spiritual and magical ability, offering a greater perspective and understanding than is usually achieved when, for example, we focus just upon the mind in isolation of the emotions, or the body without due respect for the soul or spirit, and so on. All parts of us are connected and so all merit exploration when a solution is called for. I have found many instances where a healing has spontaneously occurred simply because everything is in the right alignment to be recognized, acknowledged and released.

Our Own Nature

As our connection with nature grows, so we naturally develop a deeper understanding of our own nature. As our connection with our own nature develops, we find we also have a deeper understanding of the natural world, for the two are intimately entwined and ultimately the same.

Paracelsus, a fifteenth-century alchemist, is quoted as saying, 'The first requirement for the study of magic is a thorough knowledge of nature.' This is as true today as it was all those hundreds of years ago. Working magically and spiritually with 'supernatural' sensing, we can be led to, shown, given gifts and illuminations; we are guided rightly and so, as time passes, we become more certain because this natural guidance has proven, over time, to be correct and true.

Many of us will have had some kind of supernatural experience with synchronicity or perhaps we have felt a momentary sense of otherworldliness surrounding us. This is what I call the *feeling nature* of magic – the one that brings a sense of the expanded moment, a space between.

Where we have any sense of doubt, discomfort, or confusion, something or some aspect is not aligned enough for us to have the clarity to discover the 'one truth' or, in this instance, the particular or most appropriate 'nature' cure. In such instances, I know that the timing or some other aspect is not quite right.

In my experience, these methods of healing have historically, and time and time again, been proven to be very effective. This is why, to me, Paracelsus's message remains so true and appropriate today. It was a rightful message, and it is to five 'rightnesses' that I turn on a regular basis in my own spiritual practice.

In order to find the nature of something, I work with right involvement, right attitude, right intent, right focus and right alignment. With these five rightnesses activated, I find that truth can flow easily and rightful healing results. For each rightness I ask, explore, define, have dialogue with, test, gain knowledge of and listen to the person, ailment or issue, so that I can take any steps forward in full consciousness and with total commitment and faith, so as to achieve the right outcome for all concerned.

RIGHT INVOLVEMENT

This means that before becoming involved in any healing event I ask myself three things:

- Do I have anything to offer to this?
  (In other words, am I the right person to assist?)

- Does this have anything to offer me?
  (Is there something I may learn or be taught from this?)

- Do I become involved at all at this time?
  (... and to what level?)

Only when I have received appropriate answers, do I progress in any direction.

RIGHT ATTITUDE

This means that I approach everything with an open mind and heart and not with any preconceived ideas, assumptions or arrogance, but with a fresh perspective. I find that preparing myself through breathing and centring is helpful here.

RIGHT INTENT

This means making sure that I know what progression is most appropriate and how to progress. For example, a broken bone requires setting and possibly surgery. A broken bone may, however, also benefit from the added input of absent or spiritual healing to speed recovery. Right intent therefore means working with the most appropriate healing methods available. It also means that our intentions are selfless and that we don't interfere unnecessarily in someone else's healing journey.

RIGHT FOCUS

This means ensuring that I am balanced, centred and prepared enough prior to commencing any healing, as well as able and capable of holding clear focus while performing any healing activity. This applies especially at those times when the client may be very confused and out of balance. All involved can then trust the process, because with a clear focus I can hold to an outcome that is for the highest good of all concerned and I can remain a centre of balance and healing for the person, child, animal or issue, until the process is completed.

RIGHT ALIGNMENT

Right alignment means ensuring that I have everything that is required to make a healing go smoothly and well. This refers to any equipment or ingredients, to alignment within myself, both as the healer and with that which is being healed. I must be prepared on all levels, which means on physical, emotional, mental and spiritual levels and includes knowing the right place and the right time and the wisdom to feel for and read those moments correctly, and also to aid rightful alignment of the client. If something feels confused or unclear I then trust that either the time is not yet right or alignment is still in progress and will take as long as it takes. I learned many years ago that we cannot, and nor should we, try to push the process, for this goes against its true nature.

So how can we measure our responses and relationships to life and know they come from our 'right' place or from a pure and clean perspective? It is so easy to colour perceptions and practices through our various filters, such as 'bitter experience', 'habit', 'belief systems', 'certificates' and also for very believable sub-personalities to rise and take over proceedings.

A good time to observe ourselves is when change is occurring, when something appears to be destabilizing or altering our world in some way. It is at these times I find that I can gain great wisdom and knowledge. In these instances, we can ask ourselves the following questions:

- Do I recognize this aspect of myself? What is it?

- Do I understand the message/reason for this aspect of myself?

- Do I accept or reject the information?

(We should remember that just because we feel something strongly, this does not necessarily make it 'the truth').

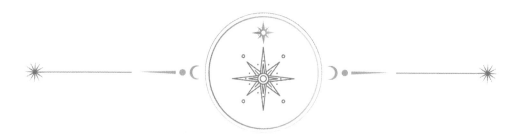

ALIGNING THE INNER AND OUTER WORLDS

1. A very simple exercise to ground, centre and align is to take a few deep breaths. Tune in to your inner spirit – your soul – and feel its presence.

2. After a few minutes, sense your outer skin, your form – your physical body – and feel its presence. Sense and feel whether they are in alignment. Are your 'energetic' feet in your physical feet, and so on all around your being?

    Then, giving time for each part of you to align and for you to feel that alignment happening, say to yourself:
    'Are my feet in my feet? Check.
    Are my knees in my knees? Check.
    Are my hips in my hips? Check.
    Are my shoulders in my shoulders? Check.
    Are my hands in my hands? Check.
    Are my elbows in my elbows? Check.
    Is my head in my head? Check.'

3. Wait, and experience each alignment. When all is in its rightful place, you will be physically and energetically aligned.

Some may say that all this exploration or involvement is unnecessary – and that one simply gathers the herb, carries the talisman, imbibes the suggested essence and all will work just as well. This works for certain conditions. But when it comes to those other, far less obvious, reasons for distress, unease or affected health, I say that throughout my twenty-five years as a healer, I have consistently found that when I truly understand the nature of whatever needs healing, a profound and lasting effect results, because it guides me straight and true to the right and most effective way to proceed both in healing and in all other areas of life. And at the root of it all is always – nature!

The Seasons

Each season has its place on the pagan Wheel of the Year. Spring is in the east, summer is in the south, autumn is in the west and winter is in the north. This is a symbolic depiction of the seasons that helps us to describe or define the seasonal variations within a circle.

As each season rises and falls, so the rhythms of nature also rise and fall within us. Our lives are similar to the four seasons. The baby, the child, the adult and the elder are like the spring, summer, autumn and winter of our own existence. Nature ebbs and flows throughout each year, bringing new life, nurturing it, providing the fruits and finally, releasing everything back into the earth. Then the whole cycle begins again.

The table below provides a seasonal example of correspondences. We need to understand the maps we make with our magic, so that our intentions and focus are clear. In spring, the most potent time for magical work is the dawn of the day with the athame. Therefore, if you specifically wish to honour the spring season, you should include dawn and the athame as well as perhaps violet and yellow flowers and candles. The autumn season involves sunset and the chalice, and so on (*see also* Magical Correspondences, *pages 58–9*).

Each season can provide us with opportunities to explore our humanity. In spring, for example, when the eggs are fertilized and new life stirs in the seeds, we can consider what new ideas we might like to bring into being in our coming year. It is the time to plant our life seeds and ideas, utilizing the spring correspondences below.

SEASONAL CORRESPONDENCES

SEASON	DIRECTION	TIME OF DAY	COLOURS	ELEMENT	TOOL	FLOWER
SPRING	east	dawn	yellow, violet	air	athame	lavender
SUMMER	south	midday	red, green	fire	wand	marigold
AUTUMN	west	dusk	blue, orange	water	chalice	cornflower
WINTER	north	midnight	black, white	earth	pentagram	pine

In summer, when nature is rampant and growing fast, it is the time for the manifestation of those ideas that we planted in the spring. The seeds of our labours should be starting to show in some way in our lives at some practical or visible level.

Autumn is the time of the harvest. We should be able to 'harvest' the fruits of our labours from the seeds we planted in the spring or, in other words, gain some kind of results. It is also the time to prune back and/or release those seeds (ideas or plans) that did not, or could not, manifest for us in that year. We should either leave them alone or plan to replant them as new ideas in the following spring.

In the winter, we can envision what we would like to achieve in the year to come. Rest is necessary. It provides a break between cycles, giving us the time to contemplate and consider potential courses of action. The more we can learn to follow these patterns that are revealed in nature, the more in tune with nature we become.

Spring

All of the pagan festivals begin at sunset on the day before the actual date and run until sunset on the actual date. At the dawn of spring – on the eve of 2 February – the first of three witchcraft fertility festivals heralds the return of the virgin goddess to the earth. Now we bless the wells and springs, cleanse and clear our environments and welcome the beginning of the new season. Keywords are purity, innocence, cleansing, new beginnings and growth.

MAKING SACRED INCENSE

It is advisable to make specific magical blends during the actual season when you can gather ingredients as they ripen. This ensures that the flavours and fragrances of that time of year are at their most potent.

WARNING: Please be aware that some oils and fragrances can be toxic to animals. Do not burn or use if they are around you, without checking safety for them first. Please do not use any herbs or oils if you are pregnant or on medication or have an on-going health issue of any kind.

SPRING CORRESPONDENCES
White, pastel colours, the veil, snowdrops, lilies, rowan trees, seashells, primroses, violets, white candles.

Direction: East
Magical Tool: Athame
Time of Day: Dawn

When you make up your own blends of incense, you concentrate more of your energy and intent into the ritual or magical event when you burn them. Because incense is one of the air element's representations, making mixtures is an ideal activity to undertake during the spring season. Spring is the time on the Wheel of the Year that is associated with the air element. However, you can make seasonal incenses throughout the whole year.

1. Gather the ingredients you need either at dawn on 2 February or in the early evening of 1 February. Decorate your altar with a bowl of spring water, irises, snowdrops, rowan sprigs, seashells, violets, primroses and white candles. If you like, choose a swathe of white or pastel veil material that you can wear over your head.

2. Set your altar in the eastern quarter of your circle, along with your incense ingredients and a pestle and mortar. Open your circle in the usual way. Place the veil over your head and close your eyes for a moment. Hold your palms out to your herbs on the altar and call for the virgin Goddess to bless your ingredients by saying:
   'In dawning Light, bless Lady Bright these herbs of spring to welcome in the Bride.'

3. In accordance with the recipe that follows, put your myrrh grains into a mortar and use a pestle to grind them into smaller grains. Add the angelica, lavender flowers and finely chopped bay leaves and continue to grind them together. Add nine drops of lemon verbena oil. Finally, add your snowdrop flower heads, if using, and mix gently.

   Ingredients
   - 2 tsp myrrh grains
   - 1 tsp angelica herb
   - 1 tsp dried lavender flowers
   - 3 bay leaves, finely chopped
   - 9 drops lemon verbena oil
   - snowdrop flowers (optional) – please do not pick from the wild

4. Pour your mixture into an airtight jar and then place it back on your altar. Lift your veil, take up your athame, place the blade over the jar and say:
   ''Tis made for the maiden. Awaken, awaken, O heralds of spring.'

5. Close your circle as before.

Your incense is now blessed and consecrated for magical use. Burn it during all springtime rituals and magical workings.

SUMMER

Summer celebrations begin at Beltaine, which is the third witchcraft fertility festival. Beltaine begins at sunset the evening before 1 May and lasts until sunset on 1 May. The celebrations peak at the summer solstice before slowly fading into the autumn colours of the harvest months. We are at the time of year when fresh, new green life is bursting out across the fields. We can now celebrate the growing time – the fertile and spirited time – that is filled to brimming with a summer's promise. Keywords are fertility, abundance, magic, growth and advancement, love, celebration and union/partings.

MAKING A WAND

When making a wand, you can shape it decoratively or keep it as plain as you wish. Since it will be your fire element tool, it should ideally be harvested from a living tree around midday on a dry, sunny day.

SUMMER CORRESPONDENCES
Red, orange, gold, oak leaves, the lion/lioness, frankincense, hawthorn, ivy, marigolds, rosemary, bergamot, green/gold candles.

Direction: South
Magical Tool: Wand
Time of Day: Midday

Observe which branch seems to be offered to you for your wand from the tree you have chosen. Consider oak or ash wood for your wand, because these are fire element trees. However, this does not preclude you from using another species, should you or nature wish.

1. Take time to search out the tree that seems to wish to offer you some of its wood. Leave an offering of a handful of tobacco, which is a fire element herb, and speak to the tree spirit of your need and intentions before you harvest the wood. Wait for a feeling of rightness, a rustling of leaves or a bird call that means you have been given permission.

2. Cut your wood. (Your wand can be up to 46 centimetres (18 inches) in length.) Then cut out strips from the bark at this point, if you wish, while the branch is still fresh. Neaten the ends and leave your wand in a sacred place for a few days to dry out a little. Carve, whittle and decorate it with crystals, feathers and other meaningful items.

3. Set up your altar in the south of your circle – the fire element direction on the Wheel – with summer's correspondences. Also, add two green candles, one gold pillar candle, frankincense incense, a chalice of water and a small bowl of salt. Then place your wand in the centre beneath your gold candle. Open your circle.

4. Consecrate your wand by following these steps. Pass your wand through the incense smoke and say:
   'By the powers of air, be now cleansed and blessed.'

   Next, sprinkle the wand with water and say:
   'By the powers of water be now cleansed and blessed.'

   Now, sprinkle it with grains of salt and say:
   'By the powers of earth be now cleansed and blessed.'

   Then, pass the wand through the flame of the golden candle and say:
   'By the powers of fire, be now cleansed and blessed.'

   Finally, hold your wand up to the south and say:
   'Lords of the eternal sun, enter now this wand of fire, bring to life the flames of light to fill this wand with good and right. So mote it be.'

5. Close your circle.

AUTUMN

As autumn approaches, the crops must be gathered and the harvest brought safely in before the weather changes. We have celebrated the first of three harvest festivals – Lughnasadh (31 July) – as we approach the second harvest festival – Mabon – at the autumn equinox on the west of the Wheel, the direction of water. Keywords are healing, cleansing, love, relationships, female issues, emotions, sleep and psychism. Now is the time to seek balance in health, heart and home. Repair, prepare for winter and then celebrate the gifts of your year.

WOUNDED HEART HEALING OIL

In making autumn healing oils, we are honouring the west's affinity with water's healing powers. Oils for many purposes can be made throughout the year from seasonal vegetation using the same techniques.

Be aware of poisonous or toxic species and do not make up oils without proper care and attention to their properties. Please don't substitute healing oils for proper medical care. Do not use if you are pregnant or on medication.

AUTUMN CORRESPONDENCES
Orange, ochre, brown, cassia bark, berries, fish, stag, grains, oats, apples, ears of corn, cornucopia, meadowsweet, myrtle.

Direction: West
Magical Tool: Chalice
Time of Day : Sunset

WARNING: Please be aware that some oils and fragrances can be toxic to animals. Do not burn or use if they are around you, without checking safety for them first. Please do not use any herbs or oils if you are pregnant or on medication or have an on-going health issue of any kind.

The seasonal correspondences presented on this page are for autumn rituals and festivals. When working with healing, we need to look at correspondences for the planet of healing – the moon. Since this wounded heart healing oil is used to alleviate relationship pains, we can also incorporate correspondences for the planet of love – Venus. Both are associated with the west. For this oil, you should set up your altar with lunar and Venusian correspondences (see *pages 58–9*).

1. Gather your ingredients on or around the autumn equinox on a dry sunny day. Make absolutely sure that each flower head and the small twigs you pick are free from diseases and pests. Gather them in a muslin bag to prevent bruising or damage.

   Ingredients
   - 300 ml (10 fl oz) sweet almond oil
   - small apple wood branches
   - 15 g (½ oz) chamomile flower heads
   - 15 g (½ oz) daisy flower heads
   - a handful of myrtle flowers (optional)
   - 5 drops palmarosa oil
   - jar or bottle and top

2. Take your ingredients to your healing altar, orient the altar to the western quarter of your working circle, with Venusian and lunar representations, and lay them in the centre. Light your altar candles and invoke the goddess of love into your herbs by saying with your chalice over them:

   'Queen of all hearts, a healing oil I make
   From the meadows of your love; do not my heart forsake.
   Be with me Lady now; send your mystic grace
   Awaken my reflection in the beauty of love's face.'

3. Place your almond oil in the container and add your twigs and flower heads. Seal the lid and shake gently. Close your circle.

4. Leave on a warm windowsill for seven days, shaking every day. Strain through clean muslin until the fluid is clear. Add your palmarosa oil and shake again.

Your oil is now ready to use. Anoint your heart and breast area before love rituals. (Do not take internally.)

WINTER

The three harvest festivals have passed. Samhain (31 October) has been and gone, marking the turn of the Celtic year. Now we approach Yule and the winter solstice in the north, the place of winter on the Wheel. Cold, bleak days – and even colder nights – cause us to withdraw, rest and snuggle in the warmth. This is the time of year to make, weave and create, as well as to meditate and visualize what you wish to achieve in the year to come. Keywords are wisdom, insight, envisioning, rest, renewal, material concerns, making crafts and quality of life. In crafting something during the winter months, we are emulating the customs of our pagan ancestors.

CRAFTING AN ALTAR CLOTH

You can put any design on your cloth, either in a central position or on one or all corners, depending upon your preferences.

WINTER CORRESPONDENCES
Black, white, olive green, the pentagram, cauldron, owl, raven, bat, cypress, evergreens, pine aromatherapy oil.

Direction: North
Magical Tool: Pentagram
Time of Day: Midnight

1. Decide what you are going to use for your altar, then measure its dimensions. Use a dressmaker's tape measure to determine the size of your altar because its flexibility will enable you to bend around and along the surfaces accurately. Decide how much material you would like to hang down at the sides and measure up, over and down from these points. Add an extra 2.5 centimetre (1 inch) all the way around for hemming.

2. Your altar cloth can be any colour so you need to select a favoured colour scheme. Most witchcraft altars are covered with a black cloth (usually with a silver or white design) when one is used. Hem the cloth and mark the centre of your material with tailor's chalk.

3. Using chalk, draw around a large plate laid on the centre of your cloth. Draw your pentagram design inside this circle, again using the chalk (any line errors you make will wash out easily). With either threads or fabric paints in your choice of colours, etch in the lines of your design and leave to dry.

4. Lay out your altar in the north with winter correspondences, incense, a bowl of salt, a bowl of spring water and two white altar candles. Then lay your folded altar cloth in the centre. At midnight, open your circle.

5. Consecrate your cloth using the following steps. Pass your cloth through the incense smoke and say:
    'By the powers of air, be now cleansed and blessed.'

    Next, pass your cloth above the flame of the candle and say,
    'By the powers of fire, be now cleansed and blessed.'

    Now, sprinkle it with water and say:
    'By the powers of water, be now cleansed and blessed.'

    Then, sprinkle it with grains of salt and say:
    'By the powers of earth, be now cleansed and blessed.'

    Finally, hold your cloth up to the north and say:
    'Lady white, on wings of night, bestow this cloth with good and right. So mote it be!'

    Your cloth is now consecrated for use.

6. Close your circle.

DIVINATION, OMENS AND SPELLS

'Darksome night and shining moon
Hearken to the witches' rune.
East then South, West then North
Hear! Come! I call thee forth.'

The Witches' Rune

When we are able to make profound connections with nature and with the powers of creation – through dedication, devotion and service to them – we, in turn, receive their blessings of clarity, intuition and increased perception. This is because our eyes have been opened to more than the intellectual or the physical alone. Anyone can develop divinatory skills if they learn how to listen, how to feel and how to act appropriately. Some will find this easier to achieve than others. You may have more natural empathy with crystals or healing, or the more practical aspects of witchcraft instead. Whatever your skills, you should trust and develop your natural abilities without anxiety about those that don't come so easily to you. They will come in time.

Divination skills are like muscles. The more you use them, the stronger and more flexible they become. Like anything in life, the more you familiarize yourself with something, the easier it becomes. For example, when someone first starts out reading palms or tarot cards, they may well miss certain things, but with practice, understanding and experience, they can become adept at their chosen skill.

In this chapter we explore casting spells, charms, the witch's ladder, candle magic and banishings. Witchcraft's magical skills require practice and understanding before they can work at full power. It is our will and our mental focus as well as the ability to conjure or feel the feelings associated with our magical intent that make the magic of witchcraft what it is. Developing willpower, concentration and evolved feelings are paramount to understanding witchcraft's divination skills.

Divination

Divination comes from the same root word as 'divine' and, in days gone by, divination was just that – communion with divine forces for guidance or insight. To deepen our psychic abilities, we should try to align ourselves with that highest source before we begin a divinatory session and really only use divinatory skills for meaningful exchanges and teachings.

AN OPENING AND CLOSING RITUAL
BEFORE DIVINATION

Before divination, perform this opening ritual, in order to align yourself rightly before you begin.

1. Breathe in and out deeply a few times and centre yourself until you feel calm and composed.

2. Light a candle or a lantern. Click your fingers or ring a bell.

3. Visualize light and inspiration from the highest source shining down upon you from the heavens. Feel your feet on the floor and with a straight (but not tense) back open your crown as if it were a window.

4. Welcome divine light into your being, as you stand in this column of light. Let it flow into your crown and down through your whole body.

5. Repeat the following invocation:
    'I call for Light from the highest source, to shine down upon me now. Above me, beneath me, around me and within me and to guide me in the ways of love, light, wisdom and Truth to the answers that I seek today.'

6. Visualize that you are standing in the centre of a circular bubble. Imagine this circle has four doorways or gateways – one each in the east, south, west and north. Acknowledge each direction by turning clockwise (ESWN). Call for each guardian and guide to come and open their particular doorway so that you can hear spirit (east, air), can see spirit (south, fire), can feel spirit (west, water), can sense spirit (north, earth) and so be guided to the messages that are for the divination you are about to commence. Say something to welcome your guides such as:

> *'From the highest source may those guardians and guides who wish to be with me for this coming session, now come close. May my readings be right and true and may they be guided only by the highest good.'*

Wait a few moments and then when you feel calm, centred and balanced, you can begin your work.

7. Bow your head and acknowledge them before you begin.

When the reading is completed, do the same but in reverse, and say thank you and state that your session is completed. Visualize each door is closing and the guides going back from where they came.

Ask the divine light to close and seal your crown 'window' appropriately, so that it returns to everyday functioning. Give thanks to all and mark the closing with a click of your fingers or the ring of a bell.

WARNING: Please be aware that some oils and fragrances can be toxic to animals. Do not burn or use if animals are around you, without checking safety first. Please do not use any herbs or oils if you are pregnant or on medication or have an ongoing health issue of any kind.

MAGICAL BLEND INCENSE

This is good for opening to higher spiritual and magical forces.

Ingredients

- 3 drops lavender oil
- 10 drops palmarosa oil
- 10 drops sandalwood oil
- 2 tsp frankincense grains
- 1 tsp myrrh grains
- 1 tsp benzoin

- chopped dried oak leaves
- chopped dried ash leaves
- chopped dried hawthorn leaves
- 3 cloves, finely diced
- Small jar and lid

Blend all of the above oils, resins and leaves in a small jar. Add the cloves and stir to combine. Leave the mix to blend for a few days. Store in a cool dark place. Use in magical workings by taking a pinch and sprinkling upon charcoal in an incense crucible before beginning your magical work.

SALLY M'S FLYING OIL

This is my Flying Oil recipe containing only ingredients that are legal and safe to use, but which, when combined together with sacred and magical intent, aids mystical and magical journeying. Please be aware that this recipe is very potent and you should not drive or operate machinery for at least two hours after use. Use for anointing prior to magical working.

Ingredients for each 10 ml bottle:

- Carrier oil, such as sesame or almond oil
- 3 drops benzoin oil
- 3 drops jasmine oil
- 3 drops lavender oil
- 3 drops sandalwood oil
- 2 drops ylang ylang oil
- 2 drops myrrh oil
- 1 drop cinnamon oil
- 1 drop clove oil
- 1 bay leaf, finely chopped
- a piece of vanilla pod or 1 drop vanilla essence
- a pinch of freshly grated nutmeg

Add your oils to a bottle that has been already two-thirds filled with your carrier oil (I recommend sesame or sweet almond) and shake gently. Add the bay leaf, vanilla pod and grated nutmeg and gently shake again. Store in a cool dark place and shake the bottle once a day for 7 days. Your oil will be ready in approximately one week. Strain and return to your 10 ml bottle. Store in a cool dark place and it should keep for around 6 months. (Do not take internally.)

Omens

The modern word 'omen' lying at the root of words like 'ominous' is most likely derived from the Latin word *omentum*, meaning 'apron'. The *omentum* is one of the body's largest organs and is made up of fatty tissue that coats the intestines of most animals (including humans). In ancient societies where religion was intricately interwoven with mythological belief, the art of reading the internal organs of sacrificed animals was a deeply respected and accepted practice. Priests would inspect the internal organs of any animal sacrificed to the gods and would predict important information concerning the future (harvest, wars, politics, weather, prosperity, and so on.). Because the sacrificed life had been elevated to a godly level, it was believed that their gods would speak through the sacrifice. Interpreting the patterns and designs of a sacrificed animal's *omentum* was a regular practice throughout Classical Greece and the Roman Empire.

Animal sacrifice, however, is not required (and would be to me neither welcome nor necessary) in order to receive signs, portents and omens. However, interpreting omens is an art form in itself.

Learning to 'read the signs' will naturally develop with closer connections to nature and a deepening understanding of the interconnectedness of all life.

For example, say I am walking along a path one evening and I glance up into a tree and see a white owl sitting among its branches. I look away, briefly, and then look back to discover no owl in the tree. Did I see an owl or didn't I? The answer is yes, I did see an owl because at first glance, I believed that I had. This is one way that omens and signs manifest – through our perceptions, through subtle influence.

Timing is another route that omens might take, such as a feather falling from the sky to land at your feet at exactly the moment you speak of something deeply important to you. There is a sense of connection with the appearance of that feather – it's as if the spirit of life is listening and responding.

Omens that have a supernatural feeling to them often happen around us. For example, an owl may hoot in the daytime on the roof of a house, or crows may caw at night, just at the moment you wake up from a vivid dream.

Historically omens tended to be seen and interpreted as harbingers of doom, largely because of a lack of education and the superstitious beliefs of the times. We should be mindful of that today and not 'overread' any signs we may perceive around us.

To me, omens are nothing to fear – in fact I appreciate them because they confirm to me that all life is connected and that whatever is to be, is all part of the tapestry of life being woven. As my understandings have developed, omens have become easier and easier to interpret. Forewarned is forearmed and when omens appear, I adapt my way accordingly.

When omens are appearing around me and I am uncertain of their message, I find it helpful to contemplate the messengers that bring them – maybe a woodpecker, a bat or a fox. I consider their behaviour carefully. Take the example of a woodpecker. They are often heard before they are seen and so I would take part of the omen to be saying 'listen'. Woodpeckers are very territorial, so I would also take the omen to be suggesting that I should be careful who I invite into my space. Basically, seeing a woodpecker would mean to me that I should be mindful for a while and listen to my inner intuition about people's hidden intentions toward me and my space.

In order to read any omens that manifest for you, you can simply 'ask' for the reason or meaning of their appearance and sit quietly awaiting the answer. The more still you are, the easier it will be to receive any impressions as to their meaning and, over time, you will develop a unique relationship to your own signs and omens.

SPELLWORK

To spell was magic! In days of old, ordinary people could not read or write. To see runic or Ogham symbols (Ogham is the Druid's sacred magical alphabet) carved into a rock or a staff covered in coded language was awe-inspiring. The 'writing' was especially powerful because these 'talking' symbols could be left anywhere by someone who had long departed. Those who could write using these (and other) magical alphabets were seen as having a magical ability. Therefore, when symbols were put together to create a spell or a charm, they were like pure magic flowing from the gods. Our verb 'to spell' originates from the same source. To be able to spell out your magic was considered miraculous. Any witches, shamans, heathens or pagans with this ability were treated with very high regard.

Many people have reservations about spell-casting and there is very good reason for this. We live in a dimension where what we ask for is provided exactly as we ask for it. We are co-creators with our universe and, as such, can rise to meet Spirit halfway with any request that is potentially possible on our path of destiny. I may well want to sing on stage, but if I am tone deaf, I am deluding myself and should be more realistic about my talents and abilities. If I ask for millions of dollars, I am being greedy and missing the point. The best form of spell-casting is the kind that calls for personal improvements, such as greater courage, deeper love or healing for others. Most of us begin the magical path by casting spells, creating charms and weaving magic purely for the purpose of improving our own lives in some way. As we progress along the witch's path, our magic becomes more and more altruistic and unconditional. By the advanced stages, we tend to cast very few, if any, personal spells.

Spell-casting requires planning, timing, ingredients and focus. The first step is to plan what your spell is to be about. Then, you need to discover the most appropriate time to cast your chosen spell. Your schedule needs to allow you time to gather your ingredients. Finally, when you are ready to cast your spell, you need to focus your willpower within a ritual. This may seem simple, but you should take an adequate amount of time to plan your spell because your words must be very precise. To say, 'I need a break from work' will bring you the 'need' for a break. To say, 'I want a new car' will bring you all the requirements for a new car, but very likely leave you 'wanting' for an actual vehicle. So be careful how you wish and read your words very carefully. Take plenty of time to 'spell' out your spells correctly!

Never manipulate the free will of others nor harm anyone else through your magic. Maintain dignity and integrity at all times and remember your oath that you will not intentionally harm others in any way. Work for the highest good, consider your real needs and remember to give back as well as take from universal goodwill by being of service to others.

TABLE OF CORRESPONDENCES FOR SPELLS

SPELL	LOVE	WEALTH	FRIENDSHIP	SUCCESS	HEALING	PROTECTION	LUCK
COLOUR	green, pink	green	green	gold, orange	blue	red	turquoise, purple, lilac
GEM	emerald	ruby	golden topaz	amber	pearl	jet	star sapphire
CRYSTAL	rose quartz	citrine	malachite, jade	sunstone	moonstone	obsidian, smoky quartz	turquoise
ELEMENT	water	fire/earth	water	fire	water	fire/earth	fire/earth
DAY OF WEEK	Friday	Thursday	Friday	Sunday	Monday	Tuesday	Thursday
PLANET	Venus	Jupiter	Venus	Sun	Moon	Mars	Jupiter
HERB	myrtle	cloves	love-in-a-mist	cinnamon, frankincense	sandalwood, camphor	cayenne pepper, garlic	cinquefoil, nutmeg
FLOWER	rose	marigold	sweet pea	sunflower	lily	garlic	heather
TREE	apple	almond, horse chestnut	plum	bay	eucalyptus	holly, pine needles	oak
DEITY	Aphrodite, Venus, Branwen	Lakshmi, Juno, Pan	Janus	Apollo	Bridget, Isis	Hecate, Cerridwen, Anubis	Jupiter, The Dagda
METAL	copper	gold	copper	gold	silver	iron	copper, tin
DIRECTION	west	north	west	south	west	north	north
SIGIL	♡	ↄ	♡	✝	♄	～	ↄ

THE RHYMING COUPLET

The simplest and often the most effective form of spell-casting is known as 'the rhyming couplet'. This is a two-line chant that has been specifically created to express poetically the spell required. The rhyming couplet is absorbed more easily by our subconscious, which is the place within us where magic percolates and is formed. This is because our subconscious responds to symbols, hypnotic repetition and those feelings beyond everyday language that can be accessed more readily by the use of poetry.

The rhyming couplet can be performed with any form of magic (such as while making a charm, a talisman, a witch's ladder or a healing poppet – a doll-like representation of a person – or casting a spell). It acts like the punctuation that directs the focus of your spell toward its desired result. The best form of rhyme is one that expresses the desired result as if it had already happened.

The spell that follows can be adapted to suit any requirement simply by making up your own two-line rhymes.

A HERBAL SPELL CHARM

1. Consider what you are trying to achieve and then compose a two-line poem. For example, 'Ruby's leg is healed of pain, she can now walk well again' or 'Sally's heart was filled with tears, now love and joy replace her fears'.

2. Purchase about 46 centimetres (18 inches) of a natural material and about 1 metre (1 yard) of appropriately coloured ribbon for your spell's focus (such as purple for luck or pink for love), and try to use natural fabrics. Gather the required herbs and floral fragrances, as well as a small crystal.

3. Set up your altar in the north or appropriate elemental direction from the spell chart, laid out with appropriate herbal, crystal and floral correspondences for your particular spell (*see page 113*). Open your circle.

4. All the time you are making your spell charm, repeat your rhyme quietly under your breath. Cut two 13-cm (5-inch) squares out of your material. Hem them together around three edges, leaving one side open. Fill with your herbs, oils, crystals and/or flowers. Sew up. Decorate the edges with the ribbon as you wish.

5. Close your circle.

SPELLS FOR GOOD LUCK

Whenever we are casting spells, they will be answered in some way. This means that whenever we ask for anything, such as success, we should prepare to have the limits or barriers to that success revealed to us. This is why magical practitioners are always very careful what they wish for. Please be aware that if you call for something you know is not yours or is manipulative in any way, you are forsaking your magical oath and things will backfire on you at some points.

HAG STONE GOOD LUCK SPELL

This spell for good luck can be worn as a necklace, carried in a pocket or draped on your bed. Hag stones or goddess stones are well-known protectors and averters of misfortune. Although most commonly found on beaches, you can come across them when walking anywhere. If you wish to make this good-luck necklace, ask the Goddess to help you find a suitable stone, or to lead you to where you can find one.

1. Find a stone with a hole through the centre, which is called a 'holey stone' or 'hag stone', and choose turquoise and/or black beads and little copper and white metal findings. Purchase about 1 metre (1 yard) of thin black necklace cord.

2. Set up your altar in the centre of your circle with the correspondences you have chosen, associated with a spell for good luck (*see page 113*). Lay out your necklace materials in the centre of your altar. Open your circle in the usual way.

3. Repeat the chant with your athame over your ingredients:
    'Lady, mother, sister, lover,
    Goddess, crone and bride
    This I make for love of you
    Let good luck here reside.'

    Make your necklace by threading the looped thread through the hole and passing the two ends through the loop to secure the stone to the cord. Thread your two ends through your chosen beads, repeating your chant to the Goddess as you go. Knot the two ends together to finish your good-luck necklace.

4. Bless your necklace with the four elemental tools of incense, candle flame, water and salt. Close your circle.

Healing Spells

Healing spells, like all spells, can be many and varied. The spell below works with the magical powers of Merlin, the great Celtic sorcerer and devotee of the Goddess, from whom he learned all about herbs, healing and the wilds of nature. He is a master of herb lore and healing, as well as being an honourable protector, counsellor and occult guide.

For this spell you ideally need a bent silver coin. To bend a coin, you need to hammer it. This represents 'killing' the coin, thus freeing it into spirit with your wish.

This healing spell is a visualization, a mental journey in this instance to Merlin. Rather than making a material object, you will be working with the powers of your mind, which is just as valid in magic as making a physical item. You may wish to record yourself reading out the visualization and then play it back. Alternatively read and visualize it at the same time. Perform this ritual at the time of a full or waning moon. You can play some sacred music, if you wish.

A HEALING SPELL IN MERLIN'S SACRED GROVE

1. Set up your altar in the centre of the circle, with olive-green candles, a bent silver coin and a small bowl of spring water. If you have one, include a statue of the Goddess or a picture you have chosen to represent her, decked in nature's finery and greenery, so that your altar is abundant with the Goddess's beauty. Set up cushions or a comfortable chair in front of your altar and then cast your sacred circle.

2. Perform the Fourfold Breath (*see page 55*) and then sit or lie down. Do not perform the breath if you have a heart condition.

3. Play back your recording of the visualization or read on to begin your journey to Merlin's Sacred Grove now.
    Imagine that you are standing in the centre of an ancient circle of majestic oak trees. There is a sacred well there. You carry a small bent silver coin in your hand. You can see that this is a truly sacred and magical grove, a clearing where the worlds can meet and merge. There is an atmosphere of mystical peace. The air is pure, the colours rich and the waters in the well are cool and clear. You look around the circle of trees and notice that before each one stands a healing being and that emerging from the shadows, beyond the grove, is a commanding presence, with flowing robes and a staff inscribed with magical symbols, topped with a large crystal ball, held in the sculpted claws of a spirit dragon. This is Merlin. You greet each other and move together to the well. He stirs the waters with his staff to call forth the healing maiden of the well. She rises on a cloud of stars and the finest mist you ever did see. Speak your healing wish to her and throw the bent silver coin respectfully into her sacred well.
    Give your thanks, listen to any words that may be spoken there and then bid her and Merlin farewell. Bow to the beings, to the trees, to the grove, and leave, returning gradually to everyday consciousness.

4. Recall your journey, reaffirm your wish and then drop the coin on your altar into your water bowl. Close your circle and leave your bowl and coin under the full moon for three nights. Give this coin to whomever the spell was for. Honour any help you receive by feeling love for the earth.

LOVE SPELLS

The art of finding true love is a noble quest and one that most of us hope will be gifted to us in our lifetime. But, many people have experienced broken relationships and very few have experienced the beauty of lasting love. When we look at the reasons for this, it is often because we enter relationships still carrying the wounds and bruises from our previous ones and so are unconsciously attracted to individuals who will trigger events that will show us these wounds. In order for magic to work, we must rise to meet it, doing what we can to prepare the way. The spell below is in three parts: healing the heart, then preparing for love and finally, calling openly for your beloved.

PART 1: HEALING THE WOUNDS OF THE HEART

Ingredients

- ❂ 1 rose quartz crystal, handpicked by you
- ❂ 7 drops rose geranium essential oil
- ❂ pure sesame oil
- ❂ small glass or crystal bowl

1. On a Friday evening just after the full moon, place the ingredients on your west-facing altar laid out in pinks and greens, with your chalice, any love items and a Venus or love deity statue if you have one. You can play music if you wish. Light your two pink altar candles and open your circle as usual. Dedicate your ingredients to healing the heart by holding your chalice over your ingredients, saying the chalice invocation:
   'Awaken now spirits of healing
   Awaken now calming all fear
   Heal the wounds in my heart my Lady
   that love may enter here.'

2. Add seven drops of rose geranium oil to your sesame oil. Anoint yourself and then pick up your crystal and smooth it with the oil mix, while thinking of your feelings and past relationships. Ask the crystal to help you heal any wounds.

3. Close your circle and then bury your crystal in the ground, either beneath an apple tree or with one-half of an apple cut lengthwise.

PART 2: PREPARING FOR LOVE

On a Friday, during the waxing (increasing) moon, set up your altar as in Healing the Wounds opposite, using a chrysocolla crystal and palmarosa oil instead of rose quartz and rose geranium oil.

1. Follow the step 1 instructions opposite, using the following chalice invocation:
   'Awaken now spirits of healing
   Awaken now drawing love near
   Open my heart my Lady
   that love may enter here.'

2. Follow the step 2 instructions opposite to anoint yourself, while considering what kind of partner you would like. Ask the crystal to help you prepare for love. Close your circle and then put the crystal under your pillow.

PART 3: CALLING YOUR BELOVED

On a Friday night during a full moon, lay out your altar as before, this time with a ruby, emerald, morganite or garnet and orris root powder.

1. Work as before, following the step 1 instructions opposite, this time using the chalice invocation:
   'My heart is open
   no longer broken
   Lover now come to me.'

2. Visualize your lover coming to you.

3. Carry this crystal with you until love arrives.

RUNES

Runes are a symbolic alphabet that form part of the northern European magical tradition. Scandinavian legend tells of the Norse God, Odin, bringing them to Midgard (the human world) by hanging from Yggdrasil (The World Tree). Runes are both powerful and uncompromising in their message. The word rune means 'secret' or 'mystery' and each one carries a specific message linked to the mysteries of creation. Linked also with the Norns, or three sisters of fate – Urd (birth), Verdhandi (life) and Skuld (death) – the runes can help and guide us toward making the right decisions and choices to fulfil our greatest potential and thus meet our truest destiny (for the Runic alphabet, see opposite).

CREATING A MAGICAL SIGNATURE

You can transcribe your name into runic symbols by replacing the letters of your name with their equivalent runes. You can then use this as your 'magical signature' on wands, talismans, written wishes, spell bags and so on.

1. Exchange the letters of your chosen name onto a piece of draft paper. Sally, for example, would become ᛋ ᚠᛚᛚᛉ, the runes for regeneration, inspiration, the flow of feelings and gradual success. This is the basis of your magical signature and can be used as is.

2. You can create different designs and arrange your runic letters to make an artistic pattern or magical shield of your name, if you wish. For example the letters for Sally can be joined to create a snakelike design – a creature I am closely connected to in my own magical work.

3. If you have designed something for magical use (a shield, a pattern, a wand or a talisman) using your runic signature on it, it should be consecrated in a sacred circle with the four elements, if you wish to activate it (see *page 25*).

MAKING A BIND RUNE

A bind rune is a design made up of two or more runic symbols, traditionally used by Norse warriors as tokens of power. Design your own combinations or make your own 'successful partnerships' bind rune by combining the 'F' rune with the 'G' rune into symmetrically balanced shapes, as shown here.

RUNES AND THEIR MEANINGS

LETTER	SIGN	MEANING	LETTER	SIGN	MEANING
A	ᚠ	Inspiration	N	ᛏ	Patience
B	ᛒ	Fruitfulness	O	ᛜ	Parting
C	ᚲ	Clarity	P	ᛈ	Choices, the inner child
D	ᛞ	Transformation	Q	ᚲ	(use 'C' rune)
E	ᛗ	Assimilation	R	ᚱ	Life direction
F	ᚠ	Accomplishment	S	ᛋ	Regeneration
G	ᚷ	Partnerships	T	ᛏ	Conquest
H	ᚺ	Tests and challenges	U	ᚢ	Inner strength
I	ᛁ	Suspension	V	ᚢ ᛈ	(Choose either)
J	ᛃ	Gradual success	W	ᛈ	Joyfulness
K	ᚲ	(use 'C' rune)	X	ᚲᛋ	(Used together)
L	ᛚ	The flow of feelings & emotions	Y	ᛃ	Gradual success
M	ᛗ	Assimilation	Z	ᛉ	Protection

THE WITCH'S LADDER

The witch's ladder probably first originated as an aid to concentration and spell-chanting because it is traditionally a length of rope with forty knots or beads along its length, much like a mala (a string of religious prayer beads). It would therefore have served the purpose of allowing the witch to lose themselves in their activity without having to count the number of chants as well.

You will be making a very personal witch's ladder here, and one that should be made in a sacred manner, preferably upon a Sabbat or important date in your calendar, like your birthday.

NINE FEATHERS WITCH'S LADDER

On the night of any full moon, affirm to Lady Luna that you wish to make a witch's ladder and would like to be guided to the nine feathers you will be incorporating into your charm. Over a period of time, gradually gather these nine feathers from the wild as you find them. They can be any size or colour and from any bird. Once you have completed this task, no matter how long it takes, you can move into the next phase. Purchase three thin cords, each 150 centimetres (5 feet) in length, in colours that best describe your spiritual potential. If, for example, you wish to be loving, creative and wise, you could use pink, orange and black together. For a ladder associated with the Triple Goddess, use black (crone), white (maiden) and red (mother) cords.

1. On your chosen special night, set up your altar in the north, with your ladder ingredients laid out in the centre of the altar. Include your four consecration items (*see page 25*).

2. Consecrate your ingredients with the four elements (*see page 25*) before commencing making your ladder. Once this is done, knot the three cords at one end and begin plaiting them together.

3. Continue until you reach the other end of the cords, leaving about a 13-cm (5-in) space between the plaited part and where you will secure your second knot. This is the space where you will add your feathers.

4. Gather your feathers up and put the ends through your space crosswise and then tie your second knot around them to secure them in place.

5. Bless by holding up to the north and saying:
   'Cords of three, and feathers nine
   this charm shall my good fortune find
   and to itself all mischief bind.
   My Lady, Lord be here entwined.'

ALTERNATIVE WITCH'S LADDER

As an aid to concentration and spell chanting, sacredly make your witch's ladder with one 150-cm (5-feet) length of black cord, strung with either forty beads or secured with forty knots along its length, moving along it one bead/knot at a time, when you are chanting.

CORRESPONDENCES FOR CORD COLOURS

RED	ORANGE	YELLOW	GREEN	BLUE	PURPLE	VIOLET	BLACK	WHITE	PINK
fire	fire	air	earth	water	fire/earth	fire/air	earth	earth	fire
courage	creativity	communication	harmony	healing	inner richness	spirituality	wisdom	purity	love

CANDLE MAGIC

Candles are a vital part of rituals and magic. They also signify the fire element and its spiritual qualities of transformation, illumination and protection. Because of the flame and what it symbolizes, candle magic is transformative, revealing and protective. It is always possible to change a situation or mood simply by lighting a candle. You can light candles for others too. Remember to repeat 'An it be for the highest good and by Divine will ...' to ensure the wisest outcome.

To anoint an appropriately coloured candle with specific herbs, flowers, spices or oils is to enhance and give potency to the effectiveness of your candle magic, the fire element and the qualities you wish to invoke. Again, we move back to studying pertinent correspondences for your chosen magical focus.

CANDLE CORRESPONDENCES

PURPOSE	Prosperity, material matters, employment	Travel, calling for change, moving home or work	Courage, health, energy, passion, protection	Healing, emotional peace, harmony in relationships	Pure love, spiritual peace, grace, blessings
ELEMENT	earth	air	fire	water	spirit
CANDLE COLOUR	olive green	sunshine yellow	red, orange	blue	white
PLANT	fern	clover, bamboo	bergamot	jasmine	white lily
HERB	sage	peppermint	basil	vervain	lotus root
OIL	vetivert	lavender	frankincense	sandalwood	rose
SPICE	salt	anise	cinnamon	coconut	saffron

CANDLE ANOINTING RITUAL

Refer to the table opposite to find the column that most closely suits your focus. If you are seeking spiritual peace, for example, your candle colour would be white. Looking down the column, you then need to decide whether to anoint your candle with fresh flowers, herbs, an essential oil or a spice – in the case of spiritual peace, saffron. When using oils, try to obtain an essence that is natural rather than synthetic. You can display other correspondences on the altar if you wish, such as a vase of white roses when working with spirit.

1. Prepare your room and yourself. Set up your altar in the centre, with your candle and anointing ingredient and a small bowl to contain it. Open your circle in the usual way.

2. Hold your pillar candle in your dominant hand (which means your writing hand) and, beginning at the centre of the candle's body, rub your chosen flower, herb, oil or spice from the centre to the top and then from the centre downward until the candle is fully dressed.

3. As you anoint your candle, you can also repeat a rhyming couplet, made up to encapsulate the focus of your magic, whispering it under your breath in a hypnotic, repetitive way – for example:
    'Moving on, moving on, trials and tribulations gone'.

4. Dedicate your candle to its magical intent by saying the following when you have anointed and ignited it:
    'Spirit of this sacred flame
    By all that's hallowed in thy name,
    I invoke thee – I invoke thee
    Enter now and light the way
    to [state your magical intent here,
    such as "a loving heart" or "peace"].'

5. Close your circle. You can light your anointed pillar candle every time you wish to reaffirm its magic for as long as you wish. (Please don't leave naked flames unattended.)

Making Wishes

Before making any wishes, it is wise to really understand the saying 'Be careful what you wish for.' Wishes will come true – no matter how long they may take to manifest – which could mean many lifetimes. When I make a wish, which is not very often these days, I am careful to include the following invocation before I cast it: 'An it be for the highest good, aligned with divine will, harming none and achievable in this lifetime ... .'

Wishing magic is most potent when we wish good things for others; which by its very nature means that whoever is making the wish has an evolved understanding of how magic works. The evolutionary magical steps are:

1. wishing for me
2. wishing for us, including me
3. wishing just for you or for all

Timing

Timing of wishes is important. For drawing something to you, such as a new job opportunity or a loving partner, work from the new moon to the full moon phase. To release something, such as an illness or the dysfunctional aspects of a relationship, work with the waning moon phase. The waning moon begins on the third day after the full moon. The new moon begins when you can see a silver crescent in the sky.

Wishing and the Four Elements

Each element has its particular associations with certain wishes. Refer to the candle correspondences chart (*see page 124*) to see which is most suited to your needs and then use the appropriately coloured candle for your chosen element.

Outdoor Wishes

When working with the earth element, you could plant your wish outside, written on a piece of natural paper and bury it beneath a favourite plant or tree that draws your attention. Do not return to dig it up once buried.

When working with the air element, consider the breeze blowing your wish by perhaps hanging a ribbon from a window or tree branch or whispering it upon the breeze.

When working with the fire element, you could hang a lantern somewhere safe containing a red or orange candle, or face the sunrise or sunset, as you make your wish.

When working with the water element, you could go to a lake, a river or a stream and place your wish within a crystal that you then cast into the waters.

INDOOR WISHES

When working indoors, light your appropriately coloured candle every evening for 7 days, repeating your wish three times to yourself each night as you light it, and focusing on the rightful outcome for you and all concerned once it is lit.

EARTH: Green candle (new to full moon phase)
Light a green candle every evening when your wish is associated with:
  Financial security
  Practical areas of your life
  Fertility and fertile opportunities
  Stability
  Home and garden
  Work
  Children and conception

AIR: Yellow candle (new moon phase)
Light a yellow candle every evening when your wish is associated with:
  Travel
  Passing tests or exams
  Job interviews
  Mental stability
  De-stressing
  Medicine and health

FIRE: Bright blue candle (full moon phase)
Light a bright blue candle every evening when your wish is associated with:
  Courage
  Removal of conflict
  Confidence
  Dynamic energy
  Psychic protection
  Passion and desire

WATER: A pale blue or white candle (waning moon phase)
Light a pale blue candle every evening when your wish is associated with:
  Healing illness
  Emotional issues
  Relationship harmony
  Dreams
  Trust

BANISHINGS

Life has two aspects, dark and light, night and day, happy and sad, good and evil. This is the nature of our duality – its purpose is to help us find balance and harmony within these polar opposites and, with this in mind, we now look at banishing. In order to know light, we must have darkness. In order to attain enlightenment, we must, therefore, understand the shadow-lands – those aspects of ourselves that are unexplored, unrealized, trapped or manipulated by ignorance (such as habitual emotional reactions, stealing or self-abuse).

Energy is everywhere, both in the shadows and the light of our being. To banish something is to command its removal. If we banish unwanted emotional or psychic energy, we should also remember to fill that space afterward with symbols or qualities of light.

ENERGY CLEARING

This banishing can be performed to clear an environment before undertaking rituals, or to remove unwanted or excess emotional or psychic energy.

1. Make a small portable altar if you need to clear more than one area. Set up your altar with one large white altar candle and one slightly smaller black candle in the centre of your area, then add a bell.

2. You will need a pestle and mortar, two bowls, a heatproof container, such as a scallop shell, and your athame. Measure out your dried exorcism blend ingredients (see below) into one of your bowls. Blend and grind them down to small pieces, little by little, in your pestle and mortar, placing your blended ingredients into another bowl for the time being.

Ingredients
- 2 parts frankincense
- 1 part copal
- 1 part yarrow
- 1 part angelica leaves
- 8 drops rosemary essential oil

3. Once this is completed, add your rosemary oil and mix together thoroughly. Place a large pinch of your mix into your heatproof container on top of burning charcoal. (Please beware – the container will get very hot underneath.) Light your black candle.

4. Walk from the area entrance in a counter-clockwise direction, wafting your herbs into every corner, window, doorway and opening until you are back at the entrance. Pick up your black candle and walk again around the room in a counter-clockwise direction, doing a banishing pentagram in each corner as you say:

    'Begone O shadows, fiends of night.
    Phantoms, demons now take flight.'

   Put your black candle back on the altar and extinguish it.

5. Light your white candle and walk clockwise around the room, saying:

    'All in turmoil be at peace to light of spirit, be now released.'

6. Put your white candle back on the altar while it is still burning and pick up your bell. Ring the bell toward all directions as you turn from the altar. Thank the spirit and extinguish your white candle.

This process can be repeated in every room of your house, office or building in case you want to cleanse your entire building rather than just a single room.

A WITCHCRAFT BANISHING RITUAL

High magic includes a ritual called the Lesser Banishing Ritual of the Pentagram, which is highly effective in removing unwanted influences from environments. It works with the powers of the pentagram (the five-pointed star) to banish from earth to spirit in a continuous movement around the star until you reach where you first started. This can be done with pointed fingers. Or, if you can't manage the movements, you can hold a magical tool such as your athame or wand. Use it prior to magical work and to cleanse environments.

The ritual has been adapted here to correspond with witchcraft deities rather than with the traditional Judeo-Christian archetypes, used by high magicians. This does not make it any less effective as a banishing tool.

1. Visualize a shimmering, silver pentagram shining brightly in the heavens. Let the star descend into your crown down to your brow. Put your palms together, touch the centre of your brow and say:
   'Thou who art the beauty of moon and stars ...'

2. Visualize the star moving into your heart, then take both hands down to the heart and say:
   'And the sacred heart of all kindness.'

3. Now visualize the star going down into your belly, still shining brightly. Place one hand palm down on either side of your abdomen and say:
   'And the mother of all things.'

4. Let the star come back up to the heart, where it expands and radiates silver light throughout your whole being. Bring your hands back up to the heart, place them one over the other, and say:
   'And the light within my spirit.'

5. Remain silent for a while until you are filled with our Lady's light. Then imagine as you open your hands from the heart outwards before you, with your palms uppermost, that the light is now radiating into the world and extending all around you. Then say:
   'Descend upon me now and heed my call.'

6. Face east and draw a flaming silver banishing pentagram in the air with your fingers or athame and say:
    'Athene.'

    Draw an imaginary line along the ground from the eastern star until you reach south. Do as before and say:
    'Astarte.'

    Move west, repeat the pentagram and say:
    'Hecate.'

    Move north, repeat and say:
    'The Eumenedes.'

    Complete the circle back to east.

7. Raise your athame/fingers to the heavens and then down to the east again and say:
    'Before me, Artemis.'

8. Raise your arm over your head and point backward, saying:
    'Behind me, Nephthys.'

9. Bring your arm back over to your right, saying:
    'To my right, Anatu.'

10. Point or pass your athame to your left, saying:
    'To my left, the Morrigu.'

11. Bring your arms to your heart, palms together, pause a moment and then say:
    'Above me shines the Goddess, about me and within me shines her radiant star.'

Your banishing ritual is now complete.

SPIRIT

AIR

WATER

EARTH

FIRE

Inner Journeys

'All that is gold does not glitter
Not all those who wander are lost.
The old that is strong does not weaken
Deep roots are not reached by the frost.'

The Song of Aragorn, J.R.R. Tolkien

Every step we take – every choice we make – is part of our life's outward journey. Inner journeys, on the other hand, are those taken to our spirit and to our soul. They represent our inner world rather than our outer one. Throughout history we human beings have ignored the message the wise ones have given to us time and time again. That message is: 'that which we seek is found within'. This simple truth is hard to grasp, even when we are not in the throes of confusion or chaos. Nonetheless, it is the truth. All answers to every single one of our dilemmas or questions lie within us. It is just a question of knowing how to access that inner world.

This chapter gives you information on finding your animal familiar, the basics of astral travel and suggestions for creating your own journeys. These offer you opportunities to explore your inner world and build a relationship with it.

Key words to connecting with your inner world include trust, faith and commitment. Trust that the messages you receive may well contain truth. Have faith that what you need will find you and answer you, and develop commitment to inner-world practices, so that you regularly devote a certain amount of time to your spiritual self.

At first, you may find it hard to trust the messages from your inner world. Test any answers or guidance you receive if you like. If they are true, they will remain so. The more you utilize your perceptions, the easier their language becomes to understand. With time, you will begin to trust yourself so completely that you will come to know that you really are your own very best teacher and friend.

Familiars

I define 'familiars' as animal helpers or spiritual allies that are intimately linked to the witchcraft practitioner by their 'familiarity'. A familiar can be a physical creature that actually lives under the same roof, but can also be a spirit presence. The main functions of a familiar are to guard, guide and inform, as well as to share their qualities in a deeply magical and spiritual way. Pets can sometimes be our familiars, if we feel an especially profound connection with them. The most important factor about your familiar is that their innate qualities will also be part of your own character that you either develop or work with – for example, if they are a dog, these would be loyalty, guardianship and love; or if a cat, psychic understanding, awareness and perception.

You can call upon the powers of your familiar as you need or want to and also learn a great deal from them. Also, consider other animals' powers, such as a hawk for clarity or an ant for teamwork. If you respect nature, all life will respond to you and cooperate with you, too.

FIND YOUR FAMILIAR

1. Set up your altar with dried herbs of horehound in the east, dragon's blood powder in the south, catnip in the west and coltsfoot in the north, then set a white candle in the centre. Cast your circle.

2. Light your white candle. Take a pinch of horehound and cast it into the white candle flame, saying:
   > *'Air of Spirit, by air you may come, if you be a winged one.'*

   Now, take a pinch of dragon's blood powder, cast it into the flame and say:
   > *'Fire of Spirit, by fire you may come, if you be of golden sun.'*

   Next, take a pinch of catnip and cast it into the white candle and say:
   > *'Water of Spirit, by water you may come, if by silver moon you're spun.'*

   Then, cast your coltsfoot into the candle and say:
   > *'Earth of Spirit, by earth you may come, if you be from earthly home.'*

   Face each of the four directions and ring a bell toward the four quarters.

3. Lie down or sit in a comfortable chair and begin your journey. If you have difficulty remembering the words, you may like to record them before you start and play them back while you take the journey.

   You find yourself standing in an ethereal temple that is shimmering and mysterious. There is a fountain in the centre. Before you stand Pan and Gaia. Pan, the goat-footed god, is playing a haunting melody on his pipes. Gaia, the Goddess of our Earth, sits upon a bower decked in flowers, greenery and oak-moss. You kneel before them and speak your request to find your familiar. Wait respectfully. You then hear sounds. As you look around, you see a creature approaching the Lady and Lord by water or air or on foot. They speak with it and guide it to you with their blessing. This is your spirit familiar in whatever form it has taken.

   Acknowledge your gift. Give thanks and then slowly come back to everyday consciousness.

4. Close your circle and find something that represents your familiar to carry with you (such as a pendant, a picture or a statuette). Connect with your familiar whenever you wish.

Astral Travel

Astral travel involves making journeys beyond and apart from the physical body. With practice and experience, astral travel loosens the grip of the physical and mortal world upon the subtler energy within our psyche: our spirit. Astral travel should be treated as an aspect of, rather than as a replacement for, real life. It should never be used to spy upon or otherwise manipulate reality. Use it only for the greater good. Not everyone feels comfortable with astral travel, finding it difficult to leave the security of a physical body. If this resonates with you, you can still create an astral room and visit it simply as an inner sanctuary.

The Astral Room

An astral room is a magical place where you can go for sanctuary from worldly troubles for a while, or you can energetically launch yourself from it into the astral realms with faith and confidence.

Your astral room must be an extension of your character and represent who you believe you are. You must feel totally comfortable and safe there.

Begin by visualizing a room that is like an extension of yourself. You can include elementals, such as a spirit guide, animals, birds, flowers, trees and waterfalls. In fact, you can include anything that you wish; there are no limitations upon what you place in this room, as long as it represents who you are. It doesn't have to have four square walls. It could be circular or bounded on all sides by tree roots or cave walls. What is important is that there is some kind of clearly defined boundary all the way around your space.

There should be one door through which you just enter and leave, then another door opposite the first through which you step when taking and returning from an astral journey. These two doors should fit securely and be easy to open and close.

Your astral room is as real on the etheric level as a physical room is in the material world and should be treated with equal belief. You are in control of your astral room. If you want to change it, you simply visualize performing tasks to do so, such as decorating it, putting up a picture or clearing away some leaves. You can visit your room at any time without journeying through the astral doorway. The more time you spend in your astral room, the more tangible it becomes until it represents a place of real safety and sanctuary.

Taking an Astral Journey

When taking an astral journey, enter your room through the first doorway. Prepare yourself for the journey as if you were going on a physical journey. Make your intention clear as to where you are travelling. If Egypt is your destination, stand by the astral doorway when you are ready and say, 'To Callanish.' Open the astral door and you will find standing stones, a moonlit night and mystical light before you.

Before you step through the doorway, you must perform the banishing pentagram of earth to spirit (*see pages 130–1, step 6*) to protect yourself. Once your journey is completed, return through the astral doorway to your room. Turn and face where you have been and draw the banishing pentagram again to seal the door. Close it, unpack if you need to and take time to arrive back in your astral room completely before stepping back through the other doorway to normal physical reality.

CREATING YOUR OWN JOURNEYS

Each and every one of us will travel a life path that is unique. It may be very similar to the paths of others, but it is always coloured by our own individual character. Because of this, it is very helpful to know how to create our own spirit journeys. That way, we can access inner knowing for guidance on any situation in our life, tailoring each journey to suit specific needs.

We are now going to establish the foundation for a psychic journey. We need to establish it, firmly and clearly, down to the finest detail in order to be able to define a 'walk, ride, flight or whatever mode of travel' in the imagination that remains constant in its detail. To give you an example, you may perhaps begin your journey by walking through a five-bar gate onto a path in a forest. There are fir trees to your left and a mountain in the distance. The sky is clear and blue. To your right is a rising hill covered in smaller trees. Nestled among these is a log cabin. This image would be your starting point and should always stay the same. Perhaps then your path takes you down a slope towards a lake. You walk partway around the lake and sit on a bench. Then you stand up and continue to follow the path around the water's edge, back to your original pathway and up the slope to the gate.

This psychic walk should become crystal clear in your mind, down to whether or not there is smoke coming out of the cabin chimney each time you enter the gate. Is the lake large and clear, or smaller and filled with reeds? Plan your route and stick to its original scenery every time you take this walk.

Perhaps you wish to discover why someone has betrayed you, so that you can move on from the experience. The key word here is 'betrayal' and so you can dedicate your next 'walk' to discovering why this happened. All you need to do is vocalize your intent to Spirit that you wish to receive information and guidance from them and that you are going to take your psychic walk to find their spiritual message.

You should discover that, as you take your walk, things appear that are not normally there. Perhaps Pan is dancing on the path as you reach it, or an old woman gathering sticks gives you a rune, and so on. Anything appearing that is different from the original walk you created will be psychic information or a helpful spirit coming in to join you.

In this way you can create your own journeys, even down to, for example, having a temple by the lake in your original plan where someone may appear so you can have a conversation. Free your imagination and it will take you to the profound wisdom of ages held within your spirit, where truth can be found and understanding realized.

PATHWORKING

Traditionally pathworking is the practice of a student taking a path on the Kabbalistic Tree of Life, under the guidance of an experienced teacher, to seek lessons, favour or guidance from particular entities as a way to evolve as a human being. I have found my own way of pathworking, which I would like to share with you here. It carries the same principle of 'taking a particular path' except I may take several without the use of the Kabbalah – questing and journeying to find helpful understandings, much like with nature cures.

Let's say I have a problem that I can't seem to resolve, such as difficulties with a family member. First of all, I set my intention to find a rightful resolution to this issue and ask that the highest good guides me along all ways I may explore.

Working with magical correspondences, I know that Hecate holds the 'grandmother' energy as the wise elder of the family, so she could be one Deity I would journey to, to seek her guidance about my issue. Making notes of what she suggests, I would then move on to another pathworking, though not necessarily on the same day.

The moon governs family and so, on a full-moon night, I could stand facing her asking for her pure, clear reflections on the best way to resolve my issue. Again, taking note of these insights, I could then choose another path of exploration if I felt it necessary, taking as many paths as I felt appropriate until I felt confident about how to resolve my issue, and making sure that whatever pathworking I undertook has some association with my issue.

With all guidance gathered together, I would then create the most appropriate ritual, ceremony, action or intention, based upon what my pathworkings have guided me to do. Taking time like this to find rightful resolution allows a greater good to evolve.

Rites and Rituals

'May the Circle be open, yet forever unbroken
May the love of the Goddess be forever in your heart.
Merry meet and merry part and merry meet again.'

Traditional Witchcraft chant

Marking occasions in life is like providing punctuation to sentences. Without a form of acknowledgement, days can so easily run into each other and become dull, dry and insignificant. To lift an experience into the wondrous – to offer initiation, advancement and distinction – is to provide colour, depth and meaning to our progress through life. This is why witches have rites of passage and why they perform rituals and ceremonies. Life to us is colourful because we choose to pick up the paints of creation and use them.

Rites of passage signify those times in our lives when we move from one phase to another. They can dignify our status so that as we leave one thing behind, we are given acknowledgement that we are stepping into something else in its place. The occasions are given significance that, in turn, gives us a sense of meaning and validity as well. They can also be very helpful in defining the requirements of completion and closing before we step through the new door opening before us. By marking rites of passage, we move through life with dignity and a purpose without too many threads of unfinished business left dangling behind us as we go.

Rituals serve the same purpose. They punctuate the years we live and bring connectedness and significance to our daily lives. They help us to honour occasions, to join the Wheel as it turns and to celebrate its turning with joy and reverence. Rituals honour and respect the gifts of creation, which are given so freely and unconditionally to us all.

Magical Naming

Magical names are an age-old tradition, ranging from the ancient priesthood to the pagan. Historically, they were sometimes used to keep real identities secret during times of religious persecution. Adopting a magical name sustains a magical identity and creates something 'special' about you when you use it. It distinguishes between the mundane and magical worlds, especially if you use it only for witchcraft. A magical name can be adopted by anyone (witch or otherwise) to mark an initiation as a witch, to create a new image or perhaps to denote a rite of passage. It chooses you and is often evident all around you even if you don't realize it. It will either represent part of you or be something to which you can aspire. For example, my name Morningstar means 'the love that guides', and I try to emulate this as best I can!

Your magical name can change as you change and grow, or it can remain with you for the whole of your life. If you do want to change your name, you can perform this ritual again and again to mark it as a rite of passage, fully acknowledged by a special event.

Names can come from anywhere, such as a deity, a tree, a flower, a herb, a mythical creature, an elf or a fairy. They can also be combinations of two words, such as Firespark or Moonhare. And let us not forget the simpler names such as Ember and Amber. Take time in accepting a name and ask for three signs from Spirit that this is indeed the name to which you are being guided.

Your name should appear in various ways around you. With the name Rowan, for example, you may be sent a postcard depicting a rowan tree. Perhaps a gardening book falls open to the page describing rowan trees. Other indicators would include opportunities appearing in your life that require that name's qualities. In the case of Rowan, it would be magical guardianship and protection. These are the kind of signs that will appear. For detailed descriptions of meaning of names, please consult reference books.

Once you have received your three signs, which can take any length of time, you can prepare for your naming ritual. You will need statuettes of a goddess and god, and a veil.

NAMING RITUAL

1. Set up your altar to the north with pictures or figurines of a goddess and a god, and with two white candles. Open your circle. Stand before your altar, drop your veil over your face and declare:

   'Gracious Lady and Noble Lord, I stand before you to seek your blessings upon the name hereby bestowed upon me. Bear witness that I enter here in perfect love and perfect trust and from this day on, I shall honour my name with love. Hearken; for I leave the everyday world behind (ring a bell and pause) *'and mark this moment with my magical name* [state magical name here]. *So mote it be.'*

   Then declare:

   'By the powers of the Goddess and the great Horned God, I now step beyond the things of this world, free of worldly shackles' (take a step towards your altar). Lift your veil and say *'and my eyes now see as the eyes of* [state your magical name here]. *So mote it be.'*

2. Kiss the back of each of your hands once. Ring a bell and then close your circle in the usual way.

WITCHCRAFT RITES AND BLESSINGS

In these closing pages, you will find some witchcraft rites and blessings that include ceremonies for children, handfasting, becoming an elder and those times when a loved one dies. Nothing written here should be considered sacrosanct. If you would like to change any of the wording to suit your own requirements, please do feel free to do so.

These rituals can provide the blueprints for you to compose your own rituals and blessings as you grow in confidence and understanding. There is no difference between you and me except in experience. If I can write rituals, you can, too!

The most important points to remember in rituals and rites of passage are the reasons for them and the kind of structure you would like. It is then possible to formulate the actual content of the ritual or rite.

If, for example, I was asked to perform a Croning (*see pages 152–3*), I would first ask what the initiate wanted from the ritual and why they wanted one. In other words, it is important to determine what the individual would like to receive from the experience. Then, I would ask about location, timing and the presence of guests. It is also helpful to know in advance what kind of ritual the initiate would prefer (long or short, ceremonial, happy, deep and meaningful, outside or inside, at a special location, and so on). After I obtain the specifications, I would plan the content of the ritual or rite and write it accordingly. You can be very specific or less so, depending upon your feelings. Croning, for example, falls under the domain of the winter goddesses, so perhaps a significant occasion for it could be the winter solstice. However, you or the initiate may prefer another time of year and this is perfectly acceptable as well. Follow your instincts and perceptions and all will be well.

The essential beginnings of any personal ritual or rite of passage are opening the circle, honouring the Goddess and the Horned God, setting the scene (which means defining the reason for the ritual) and invoking chosen energies or helpers, if considered relevant (such as Cerridwen for Croning). This is followed by a special time when the initiate is fully involved and honoured appropriately. It is then important to thank the helpers, as well as the Goddess and the Horned God, before closing the circle and commemorating the event further, however you may wish.

Child Blessings

Since the most ancient of days, pagans have called for the presence of the three Fates at the birth of each child. The Fates are very likely connected to the Triple Goddess and her three aspects of maiden, mother and crone, as well as to the three lunar phases of waxing, waning and full. They are known in many traditions: as the Norns in Norse mythology; the Moirae from Greece and the Wyrd Sisters (the word 'wyrd' originating from the Anglo-Saxon word for 'fate').

The Three Nordic Fates: the Norns

Urdh: whose symbol is the spinning wheel, is the 'spinner' or creator of a new life. Her colour is white.

Verhandi: whose symbol is the weaving loom, is the 'weaver' or recorder of each mortal's life. Her colour is red.

Skuld: whose symbol is the crescent knife, is the cutter of the life threads that releases into death. Her colour is black.

WITCHCRAFT GIFTS FOR A NEWBORN

You can choose any of the options below to give as a gift to a newborn child.

- ✪ If you are the child's parents, plant a pear tree for a girl or an apple tree for a boy; if not, give the appropriate tree as a gift.

- ✪ Gather sacred water from a holy spring in a blue glass bottle to use for the blessing of the child.

- ✪ Give a silver coin that has lain beneath the light of the first waxing to full moon after the child's birth, to help bring him/her prosperity and abundance.

- ✪ Make a posy of flowers and/or herbs associated with love to bring love to the child's life and future.

- ✪ Make a protective amulet of dried juniper berries strung on red embroidery thread, with three bells (available from craft shops) attached along its length to hang out of reach above the cradle, to protect the child's soul as it sleeps.

- ✪ Make a magical wand out of ash wood, marked with the runic symbols of the child's name (*see pages 120–1*).

CHILD BLESSING RITUAL

There is no altar in this ritual. You will need a bowl to contain the bottled spring water, a piece of thin red cord and a 30-cm (12-in) square of black cotton cloth. You will also need some sweet offerings for Skuld (see step 5). The ritual is written for a 'mother' and a 'father' but you can adapt it accordingly if you are in a same-sex relationship. If you are single, you could ask the assistance of a friend.

1. Lay the four witchcraft tools in their appropriate directions on the floor or ground. Place the child comfortably in the centre.

2. The father picks up the child and takes them to each of the four directions, saying at each one:
    'Guardians, I bring you a new life. I ask that you stand in protection over him/her [or alternatively, state the child's name] *and guide him/her well from this day on.'*

3. The mother picks up the child and the father picks up the bowl of water to assist. The mother faces north and says:
    'Urdh, (Oorda) Earthen Mother, I ask that you bless this child with your ageless wisdom.'

    The mother takes some water and draws a diamond with an equal-armed cross in its centre on the child's forehead.

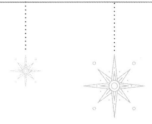

4. The mother turns south-east and says:
    'Verdandi, she who shall weave the threads of this life together, I ask that you craft a fair and halesome cloth, with many splendid colours twined.'

    The father gently attaches the red cord around the child's left wrist. (Remove the cord after the ritual and keep it safe.)

5. The mother turns to face south-west. She places the 30-cm (12-in) square black cotton cloth gently over the child's head and says:
    'Skuld, she who stands at the threshold of each mortal soul's departing, may you grant this child a full and fruitful life before you decree the tapestry complete.'

    Lift the cloth away from the child and bundle unwrapped sweets, cakes and fragrant gifts into it to appease Lady Skuld. (You should bury the bundle after the ritual.)

6. Both parents stand together and say:
    'Lady and Lord, who gave us the precious gift of this young life, in you we entrust her/his guardianship. May your blessings pour into [state name] *and keep her/him guided to their highest good. So mote it be.'*

7. Kiss the child and each other, and then celebrate the occasion as you wish.

Significant Occasions

In today's society, we can mark significant occasions, such as birthdays, graduations, weddings or wakes, with parties, religious ceremonies or certificates. Very few of us, however, still honour such occasions as the passage from child to teen or the first or last menstrual bleed. Nor do we pay much spiritual homage to courageous souls when they triumph over personal challenges with bravery and dedication. Witches do honour these significant occasions and call them rites of passage. They offer a way to acknowledge and celebrate the spirit and soul of our life's experiences.

Each of us will experience significant occasions in our lives, one of which is sure to involve 'endings' and 'new beginnings'.

The ritual below can be utilized to mark just such a rite of passage from one life phase to another – for as one door closes, another is waiting to open.

A RITE OF PASSAGE

For this ritual, you will need to put on the altar items that represent what it is that you are leaving behind or have just completed. (For example, if you were celebrating the passage of a child to a teenager, you could use outgrown toys, a childhood cap and an outdated photograph.) You will also need two large squares of fabric (one black and one violet) and two candles, one black and the other violet. Then, choose objects that represent the new phase or what you wish to 'call in'. These can be symbolic, such as a book and pen for calling in a new course of study, or a stang for a boy who is going from his childhood into his teenage years. (A stang is a long-handled, 'Y'-shaped, forked stick that represents the Horned God, who is the spiritual guide for all men, guardian of the natural world and the earth, and protector of the Goddess and her creations.)

You can also make this an occasion by inviting others. Your guests could bring an appropriate gift for the 'new you' or fresh stage in the life of the person whose rite of passage you are marking.

1. Lay out your altar facing north, with a black cloth and a black candle. Burn cypress essential oil (cypress being the tree of endings). Light the candle, open your witchcraft circle and gather around the altar silently for a few moments, thinking about the door that is about to close. Say a few words to the Goddess and the Horned God that acknowledge your/the person's life up to this point. Those present are now invited to offer verbal or symbolic contributions to your/the person's 'ending'.

2. Extinguish the black candle and symbolically bundle the 'old words just spoken' or any other items representing the 'old' into the black cloth. Ring a bell. Put the bundle under the altar. Now, spread out your violet cloth and place your violet candle, peppermint essential oil and new items facing toward the east.

3. Turn clockwise from north to east, ringing a bell as you go. Facing east, light the violet candle. Then declare your/the person's new intent or phase and welcome it in. This is the opportunity for giving and exchanging gifts. Call for the door to open before you/the person by ringing a bell again.

4. Close your circle. The 'new' items can be displayed on any eastern wall of your/the person's home (such as on a mantelpiece or in a special area) or left on the altar until the new door opens.

HANDFASTING

'Handfasting' is the pagan term for marriage. However, this ritual is not legally binding. It is a joyful and meaningful ceremony that is filled with symbolism from more ancient times. Most couples pledge their hearts to each other for a year and a day, after which they choose either to deepen their vows or to part.

There are three levels of commitment that I have suggested couples can make: a year and a day, while love lasts, or for a lifetime. I do not advocate 'forever' or 'eternally' in this ritual – it is far too long and, in my experience, has caused many problems to those making such vows!

This ritual can be adapted for same-sex couples by choosing in advance whether to use two chalices or two athames/wands or one of each, and then deciding who is to represent Celebrant A and who is to represent Celebrant B. This handfasting can also be used as a guide to write your own ritual or ceremony using wording chosen and written by the couple.

A handfasting ceremony is best performed outdoors, weather permitting, with someone other than the couple holding and guiding ceremonial proceedings.

HANDFASTING RITUAL

You will need a cauldron filled with flowers, about 1 metre (1 yard) of thin, red cord, the rings, a wand, a small cushion, a pentagram and a chalice filled with red wine.

1. Set up your altar to the north with the chalice on your pentagram in the centre. Place the wand to one side, the cord in front of the chalice and a small cushion for the two rings at the other side of the wand. Put the flower cauldron in the centre of the circle and invite the couple to kneel together at the altar, (if male and female, the woman on the left, the man on the right or Celebrant A left and Celebrant B right), as you cast the sacred circle.

2. Everyone stands and moves to the east. Place one hand on each shoulder. The facilitator of the event says:
    'Guardians of the East, I bring you [state the couple's names here]. ***Bear witness to their pledge and bless their union with your truth, grace and knowledge.'***

    Take them to the south and repeat the same blessings, replacing the last words with ('honour, passion and courage'). Take them to the west and repeat as before but with ('love, compassion and sweetness'). Take them to the north and repeat again as before with ('stability, nourishment and richness'). All return to the altar.

3. Take up the wand and give it to the 'male' celebrant (Celebrant A]).
    Stand before them and say:
    '[name of celebrant A here], *take up thy athame/wand and make thy pledge to the one who has won your heart.*'

    Celebrant A says:
    '[name of Celebrant B here), *from this day on, I pledge to love you, protect you and serve you with honour.*'

    He touches the 'female' celebrant's left shoulder and right shoulder with it.
    She takes the wand, touches her forehead and says:
    '[name of Celebrant A here], *I accept your pledge.*'

4. Give the chalice to Celebrant B and say,
    '[name of celebrant B here], *take up thy chalice and make thy pledge to the one who has won your heart.*'

    Celebrant B then says:
    '[name of Celebrant A here], *from this day on, I pledge to love you, cherish you and fill your heart with beauty.*'

    She touches Celebrant A's heart with the chalice. The partner takes a sip and says:
    '[Name of Celebrant B here*], I accept your pledge.*'

5. Hand the couple the rings to place on each other's fingers. You now say:
    '*Mighty Ones, bear witness to this union made in love and honour, for* [state length of agreed commitment here] *between* [state their names].'

    Take 'his' left and 'her' right hand, bind them loosely together with the red cord and say:
    '*In the names of the Goddess and Great Horned God, I now proclaim you man and wife* [or husband and husband or wife and wife or whatever the celebrants have decided in advance].'

    The couple jump over the cauldron, which symbolizes fertility, opportunity and protection of their union.

6. Close your circle and celebrate.

CRONING

'Croning' is the honouring of a woman when she has ceased menstruation or reached the menopause. It marks the end of the female's fertile cycle and the cessation of her periods. Her menstrual blood stops flowing from her body, symbolizing that the gifts of the Goddess now flow within rather than through the woman's form. Wisdom and understanding are the gifts that come with age or experience, and a croning ritual venerates these gifts. The aspiring Crone can also contribute thoughts and suggestions about her own ritual.

CRONING RITUAL

You will need three cords (white, red and black), a circlet made of ivy fronds and red silk poppies for the head, a pentagram platter and a chalice filled with elderberry wine. An ideal gift for a croning is a cauldron or a wand made of elder wood (the tree of crones and witches).

1. Set your altar to the north with two altar candles (red and white) and one small black candle secured into a portable cauldron or dark bowl. Place the pentagram in the centre surrounded by the cords. The circlet of poppies should be behind the pentagram or to the right and the chalice should be to the left. Light the red and white candles and open your circle in the usual way.

2. Light your cauldron candle and dedicate your ritual to the Lady Cerridwen by asking the initiate to hold the lighted cauldron while you say:
    'Our Lady Cerridwen, keeper of the cauldron, I bring you (state the Crone's name here), *who comes to seek admission to your sisterhood. Her blood now flows as a river of wisdom within. Grant her, most gracious goddess, access to your fertile lands of wisest understanding. I ask that you bestow upon her your wisdom, grace and ageless beauty.'*

3. With the initiate still carrying the cauldron in her right hand, pass the crone the white cord in her left hand. Lead her to the south-east with it and say:
    'Thou hast been as the sweet Maiden.'

    Take back the cord. Give her the red cord, lead her to the south-west and say:
    'Thou hast been as the fertile Mother.'

    Take back the cord and give her the black cord. Lead the crone to the north and say:
    'Now you leave these two behind and claim your place beside our Lady Cerridwen, as an elder in the sisterhood of the wise.'

    Using wine from the chalice, mark the crone's forehead with the sign of a crow's foot, one of the symbols of the Crone Goddess.

4. Place the circlet upon her head and say:
    'Be blessed by the Goddess, be wise and at peace, for you are now part of a wondrous circle of knowing. Let this crown be a token of the wheel of your life thus far, and this cauldron the womb of your timeless spirit. So mote it be!'

5. Close your circle, dance, sing and make merry.

DEATH RITES

All of us must leave this earth when our time comes, giving our body back to Mother Earth, while our soul returns to the Source. Death is part of life. Witches see death not as an ending but rather as the next stage of the soul's journey. Most witches believe in reincarnation, which is the continuation of the soul lifetime after lifetime in some form or other. Whether you believe in reincarnation or not, death is a powerful force and one that touches us all.

Death rites honour the departed friend or loved one and help us to grieve our loss. At the same time, we also celebrate a life and give thanks for it. The death of a loved one is very personal and so with this ritual, you can add or change any part of it to suit personal requirements or individual requests.

PERFORMING THE DEATH RITE

You will need one white candle for each living person present, a photograph and/or items from the deceased, one white rose for each attendee, the pentagram, an apple and recorded birdsong (optional). Begin late afternoon.

1. Set up your altar facing the west – the direction of the Western Isles or Otherworld – with the photo, items, two black altar candles, white roses and an apple placed on your pentagram. Cast your circle as usual.

2. Guests gather in a circle while you stand facing west. Ring a bell nine times and say:
    'Lord and Lady, we gather here at the setting of the sun, as it goes down on the life of [state deceased's name here]*, into the world beneath the downie hills. 'Tis time for* [state deceased's name here] *to cross the river to the further shore and come home to you, his/her body commended to the earth, his/her Spirit free to fly beyond the moon. Lord and Lady, we ask that you take the soul of* [state deceased's name here] *into your keeping. Bless his/her crossing. Blessed be.'*

    Ring the bell again nine times.

3. Give each person a white rose and offer them the opportunity to share memories of their relationship or experience with the deceased. Silence is perfectly all right, too. Each person holds their rose, then after sharing, they place the rose by their feet.

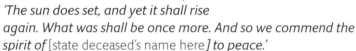

4. Hand each person a white candle and play the birdsong, which is closely associated with the journey to the Western Isles). Light your white candle from a black altar candle. Snuff out the two black candles and light the candle of the person next to you. They, in turn, light the candle of the person next to them until all candles are lit. You say:

    > 'The sun does set, and yet it shall rise again. What was shall be once more. And so we commend the spirit of [state deceased's name] to peace.'

    Place the candles in a circle on the altar. Take up the apple and ask everyone present to send their thoughts, wishes and blessings for the departed into the apple and then say:

    > 'Take this apple to sustain you. It is filled with our love and protection. Go well, fair spirit, until we meet again.'

    Ring the bell nine times. Bury the apple, either with the person or in a chosen spot.

5. Close your circle and invite participants to take their roses to the river and float the petals into the sunset while saying:

    > 'Farewell for now.'

AFTERWORD

In closing, I hope *The Way of the Witch* inspires you to follow your magical heart and that the highest good guides you well along your Way.

Here is a Celtic blessing to take with you on that Way:

> *'May the blessing of the rain be on you –*
> *the soft sweet rain*
> *May it fall upon your spirit*
> *so that all the flowers may spring up*
> *and shed their sweetness on the air.*
>
> *May the blessing of the great rains be on you*
> *May they beat upon your spirit*
> *and wash it fair and clean*
> *and leave there many a shining pool*
> *where the blue of heaven shines*
> *… and sometimes a star.*

Index

Spells and rituals are in *italics*

ACKNOWLEDGEMENTS

My thanks go to Lisa Dyer and everyone at OH!, a pleasure to work with! My acknowledgements and thanks also to P. Mills. And Mother Nature – my beloved teacher and friend, who has contributed so much to the writings in this book.

Picture Credits
All specially commissioned illustrations by Lisa O'Malley © Welbeck Publishing Group 2020: pages 1, 6, 8, 10, 20, 22, 26, 28, 32, 42, 46, 49, 50, 60, 62, 64, 66, 70, 72, 74, 87, 88, 89, 94, 103, 104, 107, 108, 111, 116, 129, 132, 134, 137, 140, 142, 147, 149, 153, 155. All other images courtesy Shutterstock, Inc./Peratek.